The Land and People of

ZIMBABWE

The Land and People of

ZIMBABWE

by Patricia Cheney

J. B. LIPPINCOTT   NEW YORK

Country maps by Stickler Cartography

Every effort has been made to locate the copyright holders of all copyrighted photographs and secure the necessary permission to reproduce them. In the event of any questions arising as to their use, the publisher will be glad to make necessary changes in future printings and editions.

Ruth Weiss's interviews with Caroline Katsande on page 90 and Elizabeth Moyo on pages 114–115 appear in *The Women of Zimbabwe,* published by Kesho Publishers, 1986, (paperback edition).

"Rhodesians Never Die," by Clem Tholett, on page 106, original ©: Third Ear, appears in *None but ourselves,* published by Harare, Otazi, 1990.

"Chimurenga Song" on page 109 is taken from *The Struggle for Zimbabwe: The Chimurenga War,* by David Martin and Phyllis Johnson, published by Faber and Faber Ltd, Publishers, London, 1981.

"The Legacy," by Kizito Muchemwa, on pages 207–8, is used with the permission of Mambo Press.

"A Lullaby" on page 211 and "In Praise of a Mother" on page 213 both © Oxford University Press 1979, and are reprinted from *Shona Praise Poetry,* compiled by Aaron C. Hodza, ed. and translated by George Fortune (1979) by permission of Oxford University Press.

"Zimbabwe," by Gloria Sibanda, on page 216, is taken from *Young Women in the Liberation Struggle* (1984), published by Zimbabwe Publishing House (Pvt) Ltd.

"At Sunset" on pages 226–27 © Solomon M. Mutswairo, is reprinted by permission of Three Continents Press which published the piece in its *Zimbabwe: Prose and Poetry,* (Washington, D.C.; 1974).

Library of Congress Cataloging-in-Publication Data
Cheney, Patricia.
    The land and people of Zimbabwe / by Patricia Cheney.
        p.   cm. — (Portraits of the nations series)
    Includes bibliographical references.
    Summary: An introduction to the history, geography, economy, culture, and the people of Zimbabwe.
    ISBN 0-397-32392-1 : $. — ISBN 0-397-32393-X (lib. bdg.) : $
    1. Zimbabwe—Juvenile literature. [1. Zimbabwe.] I. Title. II. Series.
DT962.B27   1990   89-36244
968.9105—dc20   CIP
                                                                        AC

To my Mother and Father

Contents

World Map: *Robinson Projection*   x

Mini Facts   xii

I   Introduction: The Turning Point   1

II   "Great Spaces Washed with Sun"   5

The Highveld; Geology; The Mountain Ranges;
The Middleveld; The Lowveld; River Systems
Boxes: *An Account by Father Francisco Monclaro of Problems
         with Sickness in the Zambezi Valley During the
         Portuguese Campaign Against the Mutapa State in 1571*   12
         The Khoisan Hunter-Gatherers   14
         The Cities   18
Map: *Modern Zimbabwe and Cross Section*   6

III   The Children of Chaminuka   30

The First Settlers; Great Zimbabwe ca. 1200–1450; The Mutapa
State ca. 1400–1890; The Torwa State
ca. 1450–1683; The Changamire State ca. 1683–1840
Boxes: *Chronology*   32
         Shona Traditional History   36
         Trade and Industry   40
         The Mutapa's Palace at Chitako   44
Map: *Shona States and Settlements*   35

IV   The People of the Long Shields   52

Ndebele Origins; The Search for a Homeland;
The Establishment of Matabeleland;
The Arrival of the Europeans; Lobengula;
The Rudd Concession; The Matabele War
Boxes: *Chronology*   53
       Ndebele Military Tactics   58
       Mzilikazi   64
       Cecil John Rhodes   70
       The White Settlers   74
       Lobengula   76
Map: *Migrations and Invasions*   56

V   The Horse and Its Rider   78

The First *Chimurenga*; White Domination; Federation;
The Wind of Change
Boxes: *Chronology*   80
       An Early White Settler and Her Servant Problems . . .   89
       Personal Memories—Caroline Katsande   90
       Legal Imposition of White Domination, 1890–1961 92
       Black Political Movements   96
Map: *The Division of Land Between Blacks and Whites Before 1979*   79

VI   A Short Thousand Years   98

Sanctions; Illegal Republic; The Turning Point;
The Second *Chimurenga*; Negotiations; Lancaster House
Boxes: *Chronology*   100
       Ian Douglas Smith   102
       "Rhodesians Never Die"   106
       "Chimurenga Song"   109
       Personal Memories—Elizabeth Moyo   114
       Justin Chauke Remembers Guerrilla Training   116
       Personal Memories—Mark Jacobsen   118

VII   The Revolution Meets Reality   124

Reconciliation; Unity; Inside the Party;
Land Resettlement; National Security
Boxes: *Socialism*   127
        Robert Gabriel Mugabe   131
        Joshua Nkomo   134
        Vukuzenzele, A Solution to Land Hunger   139
        The Declaration of Rights   140

VIII   Socialism Tomorrow   142

The Commercial Farmers; The Peasant Farmers;
The Conservationists; The Businesspeople; The Workers
Boxes: *Economic Mini Facts*   144
        Peasant Farming and Land Usage   148
        Tsetse-Fly Control   153
        H. J. Heinz Co., an American Company in Zimbabwe   156
        Women in Industry   161

IX   Serving the People—Promises and Problems   163

Health; Justice
Boxes: *Mapfure College—One Zimfep Project*   168
        Becoming a N'anga   172
        Witchcraft   175
        Life for Workers on White Farms   178
        Justice Mini Facts   180
        Women and the Law   182

X   Voices of the Ancestors   185

Religion; Family Relationships; Marriage;
Urban Life; Food
Boxes: *The Influence of Christianity*   188
        Shona Manners   191
        Shona Names   194
        The Bride-Price   196
        Language   200
        Traditional Shona Food   204

XI   Voices of the People   207

Traditional Poetry and Folktales; Modern Literature; Shona
Sculpture; Music and Dance
Boxes: *An Eye-Witness Account, Written by the Portuguese Missionary*
        Father João dos Santos, in 1609 of How Praise Poetry Was
        Used at the Court of the Shona King Quiteve   210
        A Lullaby   211
        In Praise of a Mother   213
        Two Poems Written in the Aftermath of the War   216
        Tengenenge Sculpture Community   219

XII   Conclusion: Beacon of Hope   224

At Sunset   226

Bibliography   229

Discography   233

Filmography   233

Index   236

THE WORLD

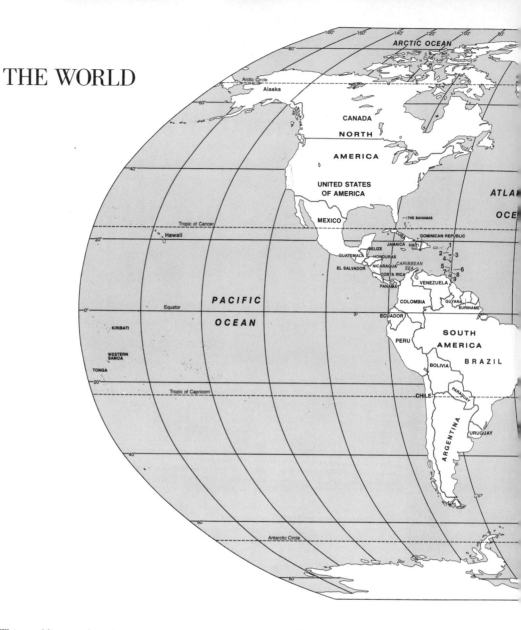

This world map is based on a projection developed by Arthur H. Robinson. The shape of each country and its size, relative to other countries, are more accurately expressed here than in previous maps. The map also gives equal importance to all of the continents, instead of placing North America at the center of the world. *Used by permission of the Foreign Policy Association.*

Legend

—— International boundaries

-------- Disputed or undefined boundaries

Projection: Robinson

0	1000	2000	3000 Miles
0	1000	2000	3000 Kilometers

Caribbean Nations

1. Anguilla
2. St. Christopher and Nevis
3. Antigua and Barbuda
4. Dominica
5. St. Lucia
6. Barbados
7. St. Vincent
8. Grenada
9. Trinidad and Tobago

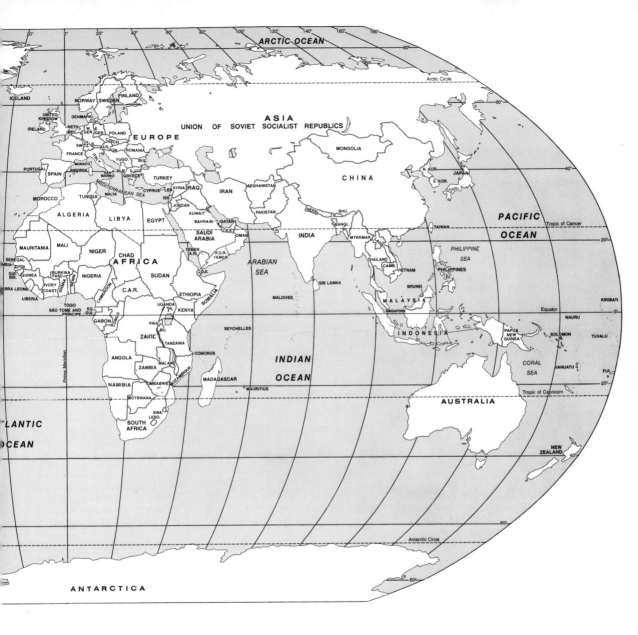

Abbreviations

ALB.	—Albania	C.A.R.	—Central African Republic	LEB.	—Lebanon
AUS.	—Austria	CZECH.	—Czechoslovakia	LESO.	—Lesotho
BANGL.	—Bangladesh	DJI.	—Djibouti	LIE.	—Liechtenstein
BEL.	—Belgium	E.GER.	—East Germany	LUX.	—Luxemburg
BHU.	—Bhutan	EQ. GUI.	—Equatorial Guinea	NETH.	—Netherlands
BU.	—Burundi	GUI. BIS.	—Guinea Bissau	N. KOR.	—North Korea
BUL.	—Bulgaria	HUN.	—Hungary	P.D.R.–YEMEN	—People's Democratic
CAMB.	—Cambodia	ISR.	—Israel		Republic of Yemen

RWA.	—Rwanda
S. KOR.	—South Korea
SWA.	—Swaziland
SWITZ.	—Switzerland
U.A.E.	—United Arab Emirates
W. GER.	—West Germany
YEMEN A.R.	—Yemen Arab Republic
YUGO.	—Yugoslavia

Mini Facts

OFFICIAL NAME: Republic of Zimbabwe

POPULATION: 8,640,000 (estimate at mid-1987)

OFFICIAL LANGUAGE: English

MAJOR LOCAL LANGUAGES: Shona, Ndebele

AREA: 150,873 square miles (390,759 square kilometers)

HIGHEST MOUNTAIN: Mount Inyangani: 8,541 feet (2,595 meters)

LOWEST ALTITUDE: Confluence of the Sabi and Lundi Rivers: 500 feet (152 meters)

LONGEST RIVER: Zambezi: 1,674 miles (2,700 kilometers), of which 372 miles (600 kilometers) border Zimbabwe

LONGEST RIVER INSIDE ZIMBABWE: Sanyati (known as Umniati in upper reaches): 318 miles (513 kilometers)

LARGEST LAKE: Lake Kariba: 2,000 square miles (5,128 square kilometers)

MOST RAINFALL: Nyanga: About 50 inches a year (1,250 millimeters)

LEAST RAINFALL: Beitbridge: About 12 inches a year (300 millimeters)

HOTTEST: Kariba Valley: Average summer range 74°–97° F (23°–36° C)
Average winter range 52°–78° F (11°–26° C)

COOLEST: Nyanga: Average summer range 52°–75° F (11°–24° C)
Average winter range 39°–59° F (4°–15° C)

TYPE OF GOVERNMENT: One-party state

HEAD OF STATE: President (six-year term)

HEAD OF GOVERNMENT: President

PARLIAMENT: Senate (40 members appointed by President); House of Assembly (100 members, popularly elected from constituencies to five-year terms), primary lawmaking body, where all legislation is introduced and debated

OFFICIAL PARTY: Zimbabwe African National Union—Patriotic Front (ZANU-PF)

SECURITY FORCES: Army, Air Force, Zimbabwe Republic Police

Introduction: The Turning Point

London, December 21, 1979. It is a typical English winter's day, cold and with the threat of rain. The streets are packed with people doing their Christmas shopping. Inside an ornate mansion, white-ruled Rhodesia is dying and black-ruled Zimbabwe is being born. The moment, though fraught with drama, is marked by the simple signing of a piece of paper and handshakes between men who for twenty years have fought and struggled over this small African country.

Mazowe, December 24, 1979. Within a clearing in the bush is a circle of thatched huts. Inside one of them, Joshua Pongweni is kneeling before a pot of millet beer and a container of snuff. He claps his hands, fills a calabash from the pot, and pours the beer gently onto the ground. "*Sekuru* [grandfather], we have brewed this beer in your honor. We wish to remember you and thank you for bringing us through these years of sorrow. We understand that peace will now be ours and that the country of Nehanda and Chaminuka has been returned to your children. For this we thank you and all our fathers."

It is a ritual that Joshua has performed many times in his life, but this time his heart is fuller than ever before. Yesterday he heard that many thousands of miles away—more miles than he, a simple country man, could imagine—it had been decided to end the fighting that for seven years had brought fear and suffering to his family. The country was to be returned to the black people. He was almost too afraid to believe it in case it was not true. Although he was over seventy years old, Joshua had always lived with the white people over him. Could it be true?

Later, he and the other men from the village sat in the *dare* (male meeting place) and discussed what it all meant.

"I tell you, baba, in an independent Zimbabwe we will be masters in our own homes again. No more 'Boss this' and 'Madam that.' There will be land and our children will go to schools with swimming pools and we'll all have motor cars."

The speaker was Joshua's nephew, Phineas, who had spent most of his life as a domestic servant in Salisbury, the nation's capital.

"Water won't jump over a gully, Phineas, be it in Zimbabwe or Rhodesia," Joshua replied, meaning that there would be no shortcuts to success no matter who was in charge. He often felt irritated with his nephew, who tended to put on airs because of his city experience.

To Joshua, independence meant more than cars and swimming pools. What did he need these for at his age? Everything he wanted was right here in the village: his wife, his children, his spirit elders, his cattle. Here he would die and here his spirit would stay to care for those who came after him. A little more land, he thought—that would be nice. He had been blessed with many children and would like nothing better than to leave enough land for all his sons to farm. *That* was how his forefathers had lived before the whites came. *That* was what independence meant to Joshua Pongweni.

Salisbury, December 24, 1979. John and Claire Wallace are sitting on the veranda of their large suburban house with their daughter and her husband, having "sundowners" (cocktails). In the swimming pool, the grandchildren are splashing around singing Christmas carols. As can be expected on Christmas Eve, they are in a state of high excitement. John has promised to take them to the park that evening to see the Christmas lights and the manger scene.

"It's amazing how unaware they are, isn't it?" Claire remarked. "This could be the last Christmas here for all of us. Maybe next year Christmas will be banned along with Christianity and capitalism."

"That's a festive thought, Mother," her daughter, Jennifer, replied. "Frankly, if it means the war is over, I'm glad to give up the rest. We were silly to think we could go on forever. At least now Dave will be safely at home instead of running around the bush being shot at." She put a hand on her husband's arm and smiled at him.

"Good grief, we've spawned a revolutionary in the family." John laughed. "But seriously, what are you two going to do? Whatever happens, things are not going to be the same here. The schools will be full of black kids; it'll be impossible to keep standards up. We might even wake up one morning and find Julius unloading his family in the driveway. Boss, he'll say, you'll be living in the *kia* [servants' quarters] from now on."

Dave grimaced. "I suppose we'll just stick around for a while and see what happens. If worse comes to worst, we can always go to South Africa."

"Well, don't wait too long, David. You and Jennifer and the children might just land up in someone's cooking pot," Claire snapped. She got up and went into the kitchen, feeling worried and somehow betrayed. How *could* this have happened? Rhodesia's leaders had assured them that white rule would last forever. Now, with a stroke of a pen, it was over. Instead of drifting off into a secure old age with John at her side and her grandchildren around her, she had nothing to look forward to but uncertainty and fear. Claire shot a furious look at Julius, her cook, who was busy crumbling bread for the Christmas turkey stuffing.

"What are you planning to do now, Julius?" she asked crossly.

"Peel the potatoes, Madam," he replied politely, his eyes downcast.

With an angry snort, Claire stomped back outside. Sheer cheek! What *would* this new Zimbabwe be like with people like Julius in charge?

CHAPTER II

"Great Spaces Washed with Sun"

In a land where it never snows and where the seasons melt almost imperceptibly into one another, Zimbabweans know that spring has arrived when pink, red, yellow, and crimson leaves appear on the msasa trees. Tiny vivid colors dance like small jewels in the warm breeze that has wiped the last of the winter chill from the air. From the time, a thousand years ago, when the first Bantu herders settled on the wide plateau of the Zimbabwean interior, to the present day when commercial farmers use every invention of modern agriculture, the inhabitants of this tropical land have greeted the msasa leaves with a mixture of pleasure and anxiety. Pleasure at their beauty and the fine weather they herald, and anxiety that the rains they forerun will not arrive.

The short September spring gives way rapidly to the oppressive heat

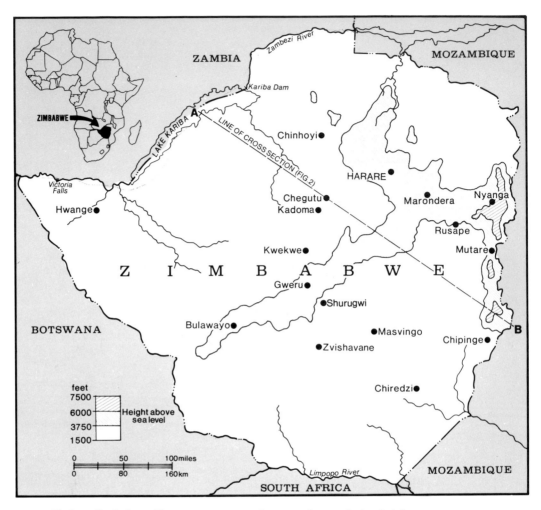

Modern Zimbabwe. The cross section in figure 2 shows relative heights.

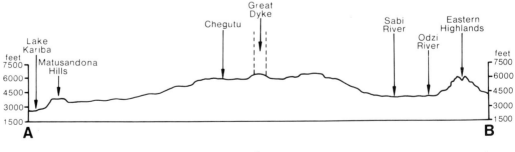

of October, and then, in November, amid fearful displays of thunder and lightning, the rain begins to fall on the thirsty land. The seven-month dry season that characterizes Zimbabwe's winter is over. Streams become raging torrents; the grassy plains, or veld, seared brown by the long, dry months and often burned black by bush fires, bursts into life. Almost overnight the savanna, that vast African grassland, becomes green, and all through the bush one finds Zimbabwe's national flower, the exquisite scarlet-colored flame lily. Most important of all, the seeds planted so anxiously by the farmers germinate, and the network of reservoirs around the country begins to fill up. By March, when the rainy season ends, most of the crops will be ready for harvesting and enough water should have been stored to see the people and livestock through to the following November.

Sometimes, though, the rains do not come. The rivers become dry gullies, and the reservoirs contain little more than caked mud where cattle stand forlornly awaiting relief. For Zimbabwe's many farmers, the result is *shangwa*, which, in the Shona language, means crop failure and famine.

This is the cycle that has governed the lives of the people who have occupied this land since the first Stone Age hunters and gatherers roamed the plateau and lowlands that make up Zimbabwe. They fought their wars and migrated only in the dry months because it was so important for the people to tend their crops in the rainy season. Early European travelers, unfamiliar with this dominating cycle, often found their best-laid plans going awry, sometimes with fatal consequences. In November 1893 a patrol of white settlers under Major Allan Wilson was massacred by Ndebele warriors when the whites were unexpectedly cut off from their main force by the flooded Shangani River.

At 150,873 square miles (390,759 square kilometers) Zimbabwe is about the same size as California, but it is landlocked and quite a

The Nyanga Mountains, which form Zimbabwe's eastern gateway.   Africa Report

different shape. Many people think it looks like a person's profile. The tip of the west-facing nose almost touches Namibia. From there to the crown of the head the great Zambezi River defines the border with Zambia. The eastern border with Mozambique runs from the top of the head to the back of the neck. Zimbabwe is joined to the Republic of South Africa at the neck along what the English writer Rudyard Kipling

called "the great gray-green, greasy" Limpopo River, and the chin and mouth border Botswana to the west.

Within these borders is a country that Kipling described as a land of "great spaces washed with sun." Divided into five provinces—Mashonaland, Matabeleland, Manicaland, Masvingo Province, and the Midlands—it rises from the valleys of the Zambezi and Limpopo rivers

Shona children take home corn through typical highveld countryside.   Margaret Novicki, Impact Visuals

and the coastal lowlands of Mozambique to a great grassy plateau—or highveld—4,000 to 5,000 feet (1,200 to 1,500 meters) above sea level. Here, amidst the rolling savanna woodland with its msasa and mdondo trees, its miles of eye-high elephant grass and its outcrops of granite *kopjes*—boulder-strewn hills—most of the history of Zimbabwe took place.

The hot, dry river valleys, the lowveld of the southeast, and the great empty scrubland that stretches from the west toward the Kalahari Desert of Botswana have always been hostile to human habitation. Poor soil, low rainfall, temperatures that often reach well over 100°F (38°C), and disease-carrying tsetse flies and mosquitoes, have all combined to

Balancing rocks near Harare, caused by erosion.   Zimbabwe Ministry of Information

An Account by Father Francisco Monclaro
of Problems with Sickness in the Zambezi
Valley During the Portuguese Campaign
Against the Mutapa State in 1571

A Portuguese force, called in to avenge the murder of Dom Goncalo da Silveira, a Catholic missionary, was struck down with illness—probably malaria and sleeping sickness caused by the tsetse fly—as soon as it entered the Zambezi Valley. Within a year more than one hundred soldiers and countless horses had died. Father Monclaro, who accompanied the expedition, became convinced that the Portuguese were being poisoned by the "Moors," black Muslim traders, who had built a number of trading posts along the river. At

keep out prospective invaders and propel the inhabitants toward the pleasant, healthier highveld that cuts a broad 400-mile (650-kilometer) swath across the country from northeast to southwest.

The Highveld

Perhaps as much as 1,500 years ago, the first Iron Age Bantu immigrants pushed the ancestors of today's Khoisan people off the highveld and then spent centuries fighting over domination of this tableland. The Portuguese, who tried to take possession of the plateau's gold wealth in the sixteenth and seventeenth centuries, were defeated as much by the hostile environment of the Zambezi Valley as by the African warriors who lived there.

first Monclaro had difficulty convincing Francisco Barreto, the leader of the expedition, that blame for all the sickness lay with the Muslims. Eventually, however, Father Monclaro prevailed, and by the priest's own account, the vengeance exacted upon them by the Portuguese was terrible:

But at last, when he became aware of their treachery, Francisco Barreto, immediately sent his captains and their men to arrest the Moors. . . . These were condemned and put to death by strange invention. Some were impaled alive; some were tied to the tops of trees, forcibly brought together, and then set free, by which means they were torn asunder; others were opened up the back with hatchets; some were killed by mortars, in order to strike terror in the natives; and others were delivered to the soldiers, who wreaked their wrath upon them with arquebusses. . . ."

Even today, Zimbabweans prefer to live on the highveld, which is part of the great Central African plateau stretching from Kenya in the north through Uganda, Malawi, Tanzania, and Zambia to Zimbabwe, and on into South Africa. Here one finds sufficient rainfall, an annual average of 33 inches (827 millimeters) in the northeast and 21 inches (522 millimeters) in the southwest, and the best soils, relatively rich, red-colored loamy clays. It's not surprising, therefore, that much of the highveld savanna, like the North American prairie, has yielded to the hand of humans. Where once great herds of antelope, giraffe, elephant, zebra, and wildebeest ranged freely across hundreds of miles of open country, there are now huge commercial farms specializing in cattle, corn, tobacco, and a variety of other food crops.

The climate is also very pleasant, comparable to that of San Diego.

The Khoisan Hunter-Gatherers

The Stone Age ancestors of today's Khoisan peoples dominated the great Zimbabwean plateau for 20,000 years until the first Bantu arrived in about A.D. 500. So good were they at hunting that the Bantu believed they had an extra pair of eyes on the soles of their feet, and their eyesight was so sharp that they could follow the flight of a swarm of bees to a distant hive. They lived in encampments, often in caves, and moved around in search of wild vegetables and game.

These people are best remembered today for their rock paintings, some of which date back to a thousand years before the birth of Jesus. The earliest artists would prepare their granite canvases by painstakingly rubbing down the surface of the rock. Later, they spread mastic—gum or resin from the bark of a tree—over the rock, which also helped preserve the painting.

The paints were made from plant roots and rocks and earths containing iron, which were crushed and heated before being made into brown, yellow, and red crayons. White clay and bird droppings became white paint, and charcoal provided black. The colors were

Although Zimbabwe is located in the tropics, the high altitude of the plateau moderates the scorchingly hot temperatures of lower areas and the humidity of the coast. For most of the seven-month-long summer, temperatures in Harare, the capital, and Bulawayo, the second-largest city, stay at about 84°F (29°C). With daytime winter temperatures usually at about 70°F (21°C), there is little change in the Zimbabweans' lifestyle from season to season. On winter nights city dwellers turn on

bound together with tree gums, animal fats, and the urine of the hyrax, a small mammal that is related to the elephant but looks like a small groundhog.

The artists used feathers, frayed wood, wildebeest hairs, wooden spatulas, and their own fingers to apply the paint.

Khoisan paintings from a cave near Mutoko.   National Archives of Zimbabwe

their space heaters to ward off the chill, and villagers in the country gather closer to their cooking fires.

Geology

Underlying much of the country is a hard plate of granite that in many places has resisted erosion and now stands above the general level of the land to form isolated hills called *kopjes*. These may be in the form of *dwalas*, which are rounded domes, or *castle kopjes*, which have eroded to form large boulders that appear to balance on top of each other. Many of these boulders became canvases for Khoisan hunters, who painted vivid scenes of animals and people with vegetable dyes on the smooth granite surfaces.

Later, the Shona discovered narrow bands of gold sandwiched in the stone. Through trade with Portuguese and Arabs on the coast, this gold brought them great wealth which led to the creation of several Shona states, loose confederations of smaller chiefdoms that paid tribute to a ruling dynasty. The rulers also used the rock, which breaks off in more or less even sheets under the action of heat and cold, to build their *mazimbabwe*, or stone palaces.

It was the promise of gold that first attracted the British in the nineteenth century, and although the country did not turn out to be the El Dorado they had hoped, gold is still one of Zimbabwe's main exports. The *kopjes* also provided fine defensive sites upon which many Shona built their *kraals*—family villages. One of the holiest places in the traditional religions of Zimbabwe is the Matopo Hills, which are the best example of these great granite outcroppings. Here, the cave cult of the high god Mwari still exists, and here lie the remains of both the Ndebele king Mzilikazi and Cecil Rhodes, the founder of the white colony of Rhodesia.

Of great importance to the country's modern economy is the Great Dyke, a line of volcanic rocks that stretches for more than 300 miles (500 kilometers) from north to south down the center of the country. In places where these rocks have resisted erosion, they stand up as lines of hills. Here many of the over forty minerals found in Zimbabwe, including chromium for American cars, are mined.

The Mountain Ranges

One of the most beautiful parts of the country is the Eastern Highlands, which runs north to south along Zimbabwe's border with Mozambique. Three mountain ranges make up this region, which is not only the highest part of the country, but also the coolest and the wettest. They are the Vumba, the Chimanimanis, and Nyanga, where Zimbabwe's highest mountain, Mount Inyangani, 8,541 feet (2,595 meters), is located. Each range is quite distinct. Nyanga, made up of granite and dolerite, rises in gentle slopes to craggy peaks. Forests of pine, wattle,

Women and children gather in a kraal *at the foot of a flat-topped hill typical of the escarpment where the highveld drops off to the lowveld.* Africa Report

The Cities

Harare, formerly Salisbury, is the capital and the largest city, with a population of about 700,000 people. It is a pleasant, well-planned city with broad streets lined with purple-blossomed jacaranda trees and red-flowered flamboyants. The streets are wide because Rhodesia's founder, Cecil Rhodes, decreed in 1890 that a wagon and sixteen oxen should be able to turn around easily anywhere in Salisbury. There are several museums and large luxury hotels in Harare, as well as a range of international restaurants. To the east and west of the city are the main industrial areas. Pleasant suburbs ring Harare, but shantytowns have also grown on the city's perimeter as more and more people drift there in search of work.

Bulawayo, with a population of about 450,000 people, is the second-largest city. It is built on the site of the royal *kraal* of Lobengula, the last Ndebele king, who gave it its name, which means "the place of killing." The city is much less cosmopolitan than Harare and is the country's main industrial center as well as the headquarters of the National Railways of Zimbabwe.

Gweru is the administrative center of the Midlands province, with a population of about 90,000. Because of its situation in a mining area, its industries include processing ferrochrome and steel.

and gum, grown for lumber, cover the foothills, and trout-stocked lakes make it one of the country's favorite vacation spots. The Vumba Mountains are known for their many fine views of the Mozambique plain and its deep valleys, which are blanketed with dark forests of evergreens.

Mutare is the eastern gateway of Zimbabwe. It has a population of about 75,000 people. Its industries draw on the resources of the Eastern Highlands. They include timber, paper manufacturing, furniture making, and tea and coffee processing.

The Harare skyline. All the skyscrapers were built within the last thirty-five years.
AP/Wide World Photos

The Chimanimanis are the most forbidding. Jagged quartzite peaks run in a barren ridge that can only be reached by foot, but on the gentler slopes of the foothills, tea and coffee are grown.

In the north, the Mavuradonha Mountains mark the point where the highveld drops sharply to the Zambezi River valley down what is known as the Zambezi Escarpment. An escarpment is a steep slope, usually caused by erosion—in this case, by the Zambezi River. The main road from Harare to the Zambian capital of Lusaka runs down the escarpment in a series of steep curves and hairpin bends, dropping 2,000 feet (600 meters) in just a few miles. Westward, the section of the escarpment descending to Lake Kariba is called the Matusadonha Mountains.

The Middleveld

Along its east and west flanks, the plateau slopes gradually down to the lower areas. In this interim area, known as the middleveld, the land has an altitude of between 3,000 and 4,000 feet (900 to 1,200 meters). Like the highveld, it is a region of wooded savanna, but because many of Zimbabwe's communal lands are located in the middleveld, most of the natural woodlands have been cleared for cultivation and fuel for the fast-growing rural population. Today, the Zimbabwean government, in an effort to stem soil erosion, is trying to replace many of these trees, but it will take years to heal so much scarred land. Those white farmers who settled in this area found that the middleveld's unreliable rainfall made it a poor region for crop cultivation, but the area has proved excellent for cattle ranching. There are several ranches in this area that are each over 200,000 acres (80,000 hectares).

The Lowveld

In those areas lying below 3,000 feet (900 meters) life is often harsh. The people must live through long, hot summers where the temperature averages 97°F (36°C) and frequently shoots as high as 110°F (43°C). Although the average annual rainfall is 12 inches (300 millimeters), it is unreliable. Some years, less than 3 inches (75 millimeters) falls. It

Baobab tree.   Zimbabwe Ministry of Information

is therefore not surprising that, except where irrigation has painted squares of brilliant green sugarcane, wheat, and citrus on the landscape, the countryside invariably presents a parched, dusty face. Intensive land use on communal lands, caused by overcrowding and poor farming practices, has led to deforestation and soil erosion in many areas. In others the influence of humans is slight. Cattle, some descended from those brought by the first Bantu herders, graze among the thornbushes, mopane trees, and ancient baobabs, which, legend has it, were accidentally planted upside down by a God exhausted by creation. A wealth of wild animals still has the run of the bush. This has allowed for the development of the huge Hwange Game Reserve, bigger than the state of Connecticut, in the westernmost portion of the country.

River Systems

Just three river systems—the Zambezi in the north, the Limpopo in the south, and the Sabi in the southeast—account for almost all the runoff water for the country. Runoff includes all the water that falls to the ground as rain and then flows into the thousands of creeks and rivulets that eventually make their way into the bigger rivers. All three eventually empty into the Indian Ocean to the east, but only one, the Sabi, starts in Zimbabwe.

The Zambezi, over 1,670 miles (2,700 kilometers) long, rises far west of Zimbabwe, in the hills separating Angola from northwest Zambia. Collecting nearly all the water in the western, northern, and northeastern parts of the country, it is already a large, fast-flowing river when it enters Zimbabwe at the country's westernmost tip.

About 50 miles (80 kilometers) farther, carrying almost a million gallons of water a second, the river hurtles over a cliff more than a mile wide into a narrow gorge 347 feet (105 meters) below, to form the largest waterfall in the world, Victoria Falls. David Livingstone, the Scottish missionary-explorer, was, in 1855, the first white person to see the falls. "Scenes so lovely must have been gazed upon by angels in their flight," he later wrote. The spray can be seen from six miles away, giving rise to its African name, *Mosi-Oa-Tunya*, which means "the smoke that thunders." Above the gorge, rainbows are almost always visible, even at night if the moon is full. Along the banks, Zimbabwe's only rain forest grows.

Despite its status as one of Africa's major tourist attractions, the falls and the surrounding area are much the same as when Livingstone first beheld them. The entire area has long been a national park, protected from development. Outside the park, however, are several luxury hotels and casinos. At one end of the falls is an extraordinary railway bridge crossing from Zimbabwe into Zambia. The bridge, which would have

Victoria Falls. In the rainy season the falls are almost obscured by the spray. Zimbabwe
Ministry of Information

Following page: *Victoria Falls and the bridge decreed by Cecil Rhodes. Railway carriages
crossing the bridge are sprayed by the falls.* Zimbabwe Ministry of Information

been easier to build 6 miles (10 kilometers) upstream, was placed there by Cecil Rhodes, who wanted it close enough to the falls for passengers to see the spray on the train windows.

A little over 100 miles (160 kilometers) beyond Victoria Falls the Zambezi empties into Lake Kariba, a huge reservoir, the largest in the world when it was built in 1959. It is 175 miles (282 kilometers) long and 20 miles (32 kilometers) wide, flooding an area of 2,050 square miles (5,200 square kilometers). The immense curved dam wall is 420 feet (127 meters) high and 80 feet (24 meters) thick. The name "Kariba" comes from the Shona word *kariwa*, meaning a trap. It refers to the way the Zambezi River narrows at the Kariba gorge where the dam was built. Before construction of the wall, a rock in the gorge caused a whirlpool that would forever suck down anything that fell into its awful grasp. The local people believed this phenomenon was caused by a snakelike river god called Nyaminyami.

Damming the powerful Zambezi was a feat of extraordinary engineering, but it had its grim side. About three hundred lives were lost during the extremely dangerous task of constructing the wall across the deep Kariba gorge. The worst disaster occurred when the first temporary dam was swept away during a flood (caused, the peasants believed, by Nyaminyami when he was separated from his wife by the wall). The rising waters of the lake also caused the displacement of 20,000 people who lived in the valley. They were not the only ones to face disaster. Thousands of animals became trapped on hills that soon became islands. But this time there was a happy ending. Over two thousand were caught and transported to the mainland in what was called Operation Noah.

Clearing the bush for construction of Kariba in 1959. Here 8-foot (2.4-meter) steel balls on battleship anchors are towed by giant tractors to prepare the land for the huge lake that was to form when the Zambezi was dammed. British Information Services

Fothergill Island in Lake Kariba used to be a hill. Now it is an island guarded by the skeletons of trees submerged by the rising waters of the lake. Carolyn Watson/Foster Parents Plan International

The dam's main purpose is to provide hydroelectric power to both Zimbabwe and Zambia. The first power plant was built on the Zimbabwean side of Kariba, and for years during the 1970's Zambia, which supported groups fighting the white government then in power, feared the embattled whites would cut off its electricity. The whites never did, but Zambia, with money from American and European donors, built a power plant of its own on the north side of the dam. Lake Kariba has become one of Zimbabwe's top tourist attractions with excellent fishing and game viewing.

Most of the runoff from land on the eastern and southeastern slopes of the highveld ends up in the Limpopo and Sabi rivers. Both carry much less water than the Zambezi, because much of their catchment area is in the dry lowveld. A catchment area includes all the creeks and tributaries that collect the runoff in a certain part of the country. Construction of the Bangala Dam on the Mtilikwe River, a major tributary of the Sabi, made development of the lowveld possible. Water from the reservoir created by the dam provides irrigation for the wheat, citrus, and sugarcane estates around the small towns of Triangle and Chiredzi.

That land of "great spaces washed with sun" that Kipling saw in the 1890's still exists, but Zimbabweans, black and white, have now left their mark upon it, often in blood and sweat. The people irrevocably yoked together in modern Zimbabwe—the Shona, the Ndebele, and the whites—have at various times in the country's past enslaved, exploited, and warred with each other. At different times, each group has succeeded at the expense of the others. Although Zimbabweans are now striving to share a common future, old enmities remain. Without understanding the history of these peoples, it is impossible to understand the modern state.

The Children of Chaminuka

If visitors from modern-day America could journey back to the fifteenth-century court at Great Zimbabwe, they probably would be amazed. Perhaps expecting to find a club-wielding chieftain ruling a band of naked warriors, they instead find themselves before a city of great stone walls. As they approach the ungated entrance, their gaze alights on six soapstone birds that seem to stretch skyward from their pedestals. A doorkeeper ushers them through a maze of passages and past a stone cone-shaped tower to an elaborately painted clay hut decorated with elegant ceramics, Chinese porcelain, Persian rugs, and magnificent wooden carvings and sculptures covered with sheets of gold and copper.

Forced to their knees, the travelers face an impressive figure, dressed

The conical tower at Great Zimbabwe. This photograph was taken during the first archeo-logical excavations of David Randall-MacIver in 1906. National Archives of Zimbabwe

Chronology

about 30,000 B.C.	Stone Age Khoisan hunters and gatherers settle on Zimbabwean plateau
about A.D. 500	First Bantu-speaking people arrive
about A.D. 1000	Bantu-speaking Shona ethnic group takes control of plateau
about 1200	Zimbabwe state, centered at Great Zimbabwe, established in southeast of plateau
about 1400	Mutapa state established in north
about 1450	Great Zimbabwe abandoned; Torwa state, centered at Khami in southwest of plateau, arises

in a single length of fine cotton, weighed down with gold and copper jewelry, and holding a symbolic copper spear. This is the ruler of Great Zimbabwe. At his side are a bevy of nobles dressed in exotic robes of silk and satin brought from India by Muslim Arab and Swahili traders.

The King wants to know why the strangers have journeyed so far, through steamy coastal forests and over mountains, and endured so many hazards to visit his court. Are they looking for gold or ivory, ostrich feathers or copper? What do they bring with them?

If the travelers act prudently and convince the King that their intentions are friendly, they may find themselves housed in a round hut with a thatched roof and thick walls of *daga*—a mud compound—polished

1505	Portuguese set up trading station at Sofala on Mozambique coast
1514	Portuguese *degradado* Antonio Fernandes travels to Mutapa court, the first European to set foot in modern-day boundaries of Zimbabwe
1629	Mutapa state falls under Portuguese domination
about 1680	Changamire state formed under Dombo in northeast of plateau
1683	Changamire, supported by Rozvi warriors, absorbs Torwa state
1693	Changamire expels Portuguese from plateau
about 1700	Munhumutapa moves kingdom to Portuguese-dominated territory east of modern-day borders of Zimbabwe

to shiny smoothness. They are fed well, too, on beef and antelope culled from the herds roaming the grassy plains far beyond the city limits. Each day, a woman clad in a small skin apron and dozens of copper wire bracelets and anklets brings a clay pot filled with beer made from the millet grown in fields she walks miles each day to tend.

As time passes, the strangers observe how the life of Great Zimbabwe extends hundreds of miles beyond the dusty city limits. The women tell of their husbands, who are far away tending the great herds of royal cattle or collecting tribute from villages many days' travel away. Among those who stay at home are the craftsmen who make jewelry and simple tools from gold, copper, and iron, and carry on the monumental task of building the great granite walls that will, five hundred years later, hint at the glorious past of Zimbabwe's Shona-speaking peoples.

The First Settlers

In about the fifth century A.D., when the Vandals were sacking Rome and the Mayans were building their pyramid temples in Mexico, the first Bantu migrants began sifting southward in small family groups from the basin of the Congo River in modern-day Zaire. Bantu refers not to a race or ethnic group, but to a group of over four hundred languages spoken by the many negroid peoples who populate Africa south of the Sahara. These languages are as closely related as European Romance languages such as French, Italian, Spanish, and Portuguese.

The Bantu migration, which lasted over a thousand years, was one of the largest mass population movements in the history of the world, and it was this great wave that brought the earliest forebears of today's Shona-speaking Zimbabweans to southern Africa. (Like Bantu, Shona refers to a collection of dialects within one language group.) The first Bantu settlers on the plateau were farmers as well as hunters, and over a period of several hundred years, they drove out the Stone Age Khoisan hunters and gatherers who had long inhabited the plateau.

By A.D. 1000 the ancestors of today's Shona, the majority ethnic group in Zimbabwe, had taken control of the pleasant tableland between the Zambezi and Limpopo rivers. Because there are no written records of life on the plateau until the Portuguese arrived in the sixteenth century, we can only turn to archaeology and the oral traditions of the Shona themselves to re-create the early history of these people. It is a confusing picture. The Shona remember their past in terms of individual clan groups rather than as a unified people, because it is only in the past century that they have thought of themselves as one

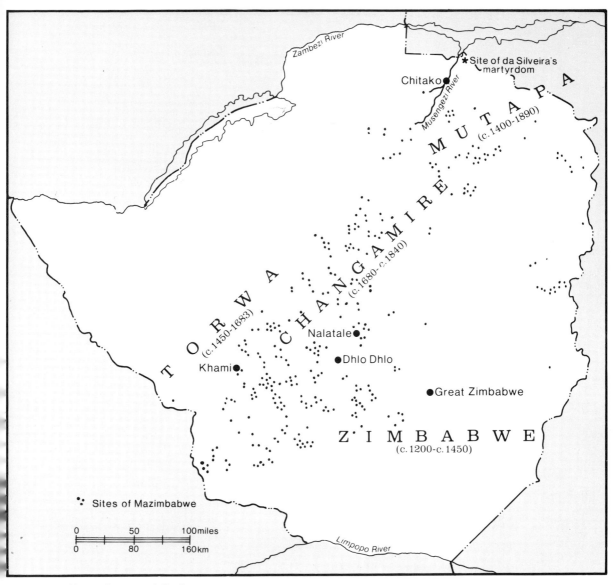

Shona States and Settlements

national group. Before that, the people identified with their extended family, which was represented by a totem or clan name. Under the totem system, each person inherited a *mutupo*, or totem, from his or

Shona Traditional History

Because the Shona never developed a system of writing, they have a very strong oral tradition. The historian might be a village elder or perhaps the *svikiro*, a male or female spirit medium, who must know everything there is to know about the particular spirit possessing him or her to be considered genuine.

Shona traditions basically revolve around genealogical relationships and land rights. All Shona children soon have an intricate knowledge of the lineages of their mothers and fathers. By the time they are teenagers, they will understand their relationships to their neighbors and why property boundaries are where they are, and even have some idea of where their family groups came from and how they came to be where they are now.

There are many hundreds of traditional histories dealing with single family groups and dynasties. Almost all have the same structure:

· Where the group came from originally. This is always described in vague terms, such as *tanganyika*, "beginning land," or *guruuswa*, "the place of long grass"

· How they journeyed to the new land

· How they conquered the new land

· Who the rulers were, how they came to succeed each other, and what challenges they had to face over their ownership of the land.

Certain myths tend to creep into the history; these are used to illustrate important points in the story or to explain certain features of the genealogy. For example, one tradition holds that when the ruler Mutota died, it was found that his body was too heavy to be lifted onto its funeral bier. Mutota's chief wife then "revealed" that if one of his sons were to have ritual intercourse with his half sister, Nyamahita, he would be given the strength to raise the corpse and thus become the next king. The only one to do it was Matope, and he, together with Nyamahita, went on to a glorious reign. It is possible that early Shona rulers practiced incest and this myth grew up in later generations to "explain" what later became a major taboo in Shona society.

Shona traditions have been very valuable to modern historians, but they obviously have their limitations:

· The teller will sometimes exaggerate or manipulate a tradition to suit present circumstances. For example, neighboring villages involved in a property dispute might give exactly opposite accounts of the same event.

· Because of the great time span covered, oral traditions tend to telescope history, often with several rulers identified under one name.

· The lives of important figures and the mediums their spirits later possess often become confused.

· Oral traditions tend to deal with chiefs; thus over time women and ordinary people are forgotten.

her father. Usually these were based on animals or parts of the body: for example, a person might be of the *nzou*, or elephant, totem, or the *moyo*, or heart, totem. Sometimes a person would add a *chidawo*, or praise name, to the *mutupo*, and in this way various branches of a particular totem became distinguished from others. The totem system is still used in Zimbabwe.

Despite this, there are some traditions that have been embraced by the Shona as a whole. One of them holds that among the earliest ancestral families to cross the Zambezi was one headed by Murenga Sororenzou, whose children included Chaminuka, Runji, Mushavutu, and Nehanda. To understand the Shona people, one must understand how closely their history and religion are intertwined. Their ancestors, they believe, are as much a part of the present as they are of the past. It is the ancestral spirits who look after the well-being of their descendants. Just as in life people occupy different places in a social scale, so too are the ancestral spirits ranked in the spirit world. A *mhondoro* is the spirit of the founder of a clan, and a *mudzimu* is the spirit of the father or grandfather of a living person. Some spirits, however, have been adopted by all the Shona people. These are the "super-*mhondoro*," who are responsible for the people as a whole. Chaminuka is the greatest of the super-*mhondoro*. His sister, Nehanda, is also greatly revered. The traditions hold that she died before the family crossed the Zambezi and her spirit took possession of a *svikiro*—medium—who took up a wooden rod and, like a Bantu Moses, parted the mighty river, allowing the family to cross.

The mosaic of Shona histories dealing with the struggles between families over the land and resources of the plateau can be compared to stories of the settling of the American West by hundreds of immigrant families. Some accounts of the westward expansion are still remembered, but others have sunk into oblivion as the families have died out or split up, or have simply been forgotten. In the same way, many of the pieces of the Shona mosaic are missing. Historians have, however, been able to deduce that certain families gained enough wealth and power to win control of large parts of the country. Within these Shona "states," the smaller chiefdoms were forced to pay tribute (somewhat like a tax) to these ruling dynasties, send young men to fight in their armies, and build their *mazimbabwe.* The first of these was centered at Great Zimbabwe.

Great Zimbabwe, about 1200–about 1450

The people who built Great Zimbabwe first settled in the southeastern middleveld because it was an ideal situation for breeding cattle, traditionally a sign of wealth among the Shona. In the summer the herds were kept on the highveld, where the higher rainfall ensured lush pasturage, and in the winter they were driven into the lowveld to browse off the scrub. Over time one clan built up a bigger herd than anyone else in the area and began to exert its power over the other chiefdoms by forcing them to give it cattle as a sign of loyalty.

Sometime after 1100 this new ruling dynasty built up enough power to take control of the important trade route between the gold fields of the southwest and the coast, extending its influence over hundreds of miles. As a sign of their power and prestige, the rulers began to build Great Zimbabwe. It was a symbol that was copied by lesser chiefs over the next few centuries. Remains of these smaller *mazimbabwe* can be found all over the plateau, but none comes close to the grandeur of Great Zimbabwe.

Archeologists think that construction began on Great Zimbabwe in the thirteenth century. It was never meant to keep out invaders but was

Trade and Industry

Despite its inland location, the people who lived on the plateau have always been great traders. These are some of the main products they exchanged.

Exports

Gold: This was the single most important export from the plateau and was extracted by the Shona with great difficulty. Those rulers who controlled either the mines or the trading routes between the coast and those mines became very wealthy and very powerful.

Whole villages were involved in mining, washing, and milling the gold. In the dry season, families would gather at pools of gold-bearing rivers and wash the gravel on the riverbed for gold. Mining gold from reefs was much more dangerous. To construct tunnels to the veins of gold, they weakened the rock with fire and split it with iron wedges. The stone was then carried to the surface, where it was broken and ground into powder before it was washed to extract the gold.

Ivory: The ivory trade eventually overtook the gold trade in importance for the people of the plateau. Like gold, ivory was not

purely a "prestige project." Great curving walls appear to grow out of the rock *kopjes* and hill slopes so that the city seems part of the natural landscape. A tower and platforms were built inside the enclosure. On

easy to obtain. Elephants were trapped in pits, speared from trees, or even hamstrung by daring hunters who sneaked up from behind.

Other minor exports included copper and ostrich feathers. Luckily for the inhabitants of the plateau, the hostile Zambezi Valley and the arrival of the fierce Ndebele warriors discouraged outside slave traders from coming into the region and taking captives.

Imports

Beads: As far back as A.D. 700, people of the plateau imported glass beads. They were carefully passed from village to village and were very expensive. Later, Arab and Portuguese traders traded them for gold and ivory. Portuguese documents indicate that there were bead "fads" among the Shona and a trader had to be on his toes not to get caught with stock that was no longer fashionable.

Cloth: Cloth was the principal import of the plateau. Dyed and embroidered silk, satin, and damask were imported from India as well as the techniques of spinning and weaving. As local weavers became more proficient at their craft, Muslim importers found they had to unravel the thread from Indian cloth and reweave it more closely to bring the cloth up to the standard of the plain locally woven fabric, made from wild cotton.

these platforms and at the gateways the distinctive Zimbabwe birds, now the national emblem, were erected atop wooden and stone posts. The birds, eight of which were found in the ruins, are described by the

Shona as *shirichena,* "the bird of bright plumage," or *Shiri ya Mwari,* "the Bird of God." They are believed to have represented the ancestral link to the heavens.

No one knows who the ruling dynasty at Great Zimbabwe was, or why, in about 1450, it suddenly abandoned the city. Historians speculate the people left the great walled complex because the land around it could no longer support the enormous population that lived there. Because of the traditional method of cultivation, which involved using a piece of land for only two or three years until it was exhausted and then moving on to a fresh piece, the women of Great Zimbabwe, who like their modern descendants did most of the farming, would have had to walk farther and farther each year to tend their crops. The people would also have had to go increasingly longer distances to find firewood, pasturage for their animals, and game to hunt. Perhaps a drought finally forced the people to leave Great Zimbabwe and go in search of new territory.

The Mutapa State, about 1400–1890

The Mutapa state arose in an area in the northeast of the plateau populated by a people known as the Karanga. Over time, they had come to be dominated by a dynasty that had adopted the title of Mutapa, or Munhumutapa, as it is sometimes called. More is known about these people than about any other pre-nineteenth century Shona culture because the Portuguese traded with and were intimately involved with the Mutapas for almost two centuries.

In 1505 the Portuguese set up a trading station at Sofala, near modern-day Beira on the Mozambique coast. Excited by the tales, heard

One of the soapstone birds found at Great Zimbabwe. Zimbabwe Ministry of Information

The Mutapa's Palace at Chitako

(Account by Portuguese chronicler, Antonio Bocarro)

The dwelling in which the Monomatapa resides is very large and is composed of many houses surrounded by a great wooden fence, within which there are three dwellings, one for his own person, one for the queen, and another for his servants who wait upon him within doors. There are three doors opening upon a great courtyard, one for the service of the queen, beyond which no man may pass, but only women, another for his kitchen, only entered by his cooks, who are two young men from among the principal lords of his kingdom, his relations in whom he has most confidence, and the lads who serve in the kitchen, who are also nobles between fifteen and twenty years of age. These are also employed to lay the food when the king wishes to eat, which they spread upon the ground, upon a carpet or mat, with muslin extended above, and many different kinds of meat are set before him, all roasted or boiled, such as hens, pigeons, partridges, capons, sheep, venison, hares, rabbits, cows, rats, and other game, of which, after the king has eaten, a portion is given to some of his servants who are always provided from his table.

The third door leads to the king's apartments, which none may enter but the young nobles who serve him within doors, who are all from fifteen to twenty years of age and are called massacoriras, *and the sons of the nobles of his kingdoms and have their captain who looks after and commands them. When they are twenty years of age, and upwards, they are withdrawn from the service of the king within doors, and others put in their place. The reason for this is that the king will not be served by those who know a woman, but only by these youths, who are enjoined to observe chastity so long as they serve the king, and if any one is found guilty of the opposite vice he is severely punished and expelled from the king's service.*

LE GRAND ROY   **MONO-MOTAPA —**

A romanticized Portuguese portrait of a Mutapa. The artist, who probably never saw the ruler, gave him the customary crown and scepter carried by European monarchs to make him appear more familiar to the Portuguese.   National Archives of Zimbabwe

from Muslim traders, of the great gold fields to be found in the interior, King Manuel I of Portugal sent an emissary to visit the Mutapa in person. That man, the first European to ever set foot in Zimbabwe, was Antonio Fernandes, a *degradado*, or convict, who undertook the dangerous journey in the hope of being pardoned. In about 1513 he reached the Karanga court at Chitako and met the reigning Mutapa, Chikuyo Chisamarengu.

After giving Chikuyo a gift of muzzle-loading rifles, Fernandes was allowed to journey throughout the Mutapa's country. One chief, he wrote, "mines a great deal of gold throughout his land, and this man saw it being drawn and he says it can be seen where the gold lies because a herb like clover grows over it and that the greatest he saw mined in one day was a large basket full of bars the size of a finger and large nuggets." The *degradado* obviously exaggerated the wealth of the Mutapa because it was in his interest to tell his masters what they wanted to hear. He was right, King Manuel not only allowed him to go free, he also knighted him and gave him a gift of two oxen.

By the mid-sixteenth century, the Portuguese were well established at the court of the Mutapa. From their accounts we learn of a highly structured society, based on a complex religion and supported by an army of 100,000 soldiers, some apparently women.

An elaborate ritual ruled the court, which had all the rigid formality of any European court of the day. In much the same way that courtiers at Versailles vied to personally attend to the needs of King Louis XIV, so too did the Karanga courtiers compete for titles roughly translated

The martyrdom of Father Dom Goncalo da Silveira by the Mutapa Nogomo in 1561. Da Silveira was the first person to preach Christianity to the Shona. He was killed by Nogomo after the Mutapa became convinced that the priest had bewitched him. National Archives of Zimbabwe

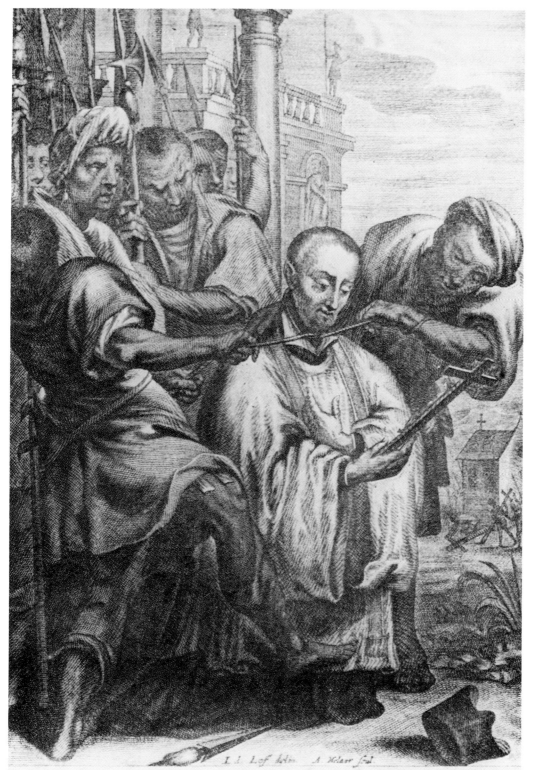

P. GONSALVVS SYLVEIRA *vande Societeyt* IESV, *wort voor*
het gheloof verworght vande MOOREN *in* MONOMOTAPA.

I.d. Leef delin.   A. Melarr fcal.

as "The King's Right Hand," "Keeper of the Royal Relics," and "Majordomo." Upon observing these aristocrats, one Portuguese admiringly wrote that "whereas the Moores of Africa and Arabia draw their words out of the throat as if they would vomite, these pronounce their words with the end of the tongue and lips, that they speak many words in a whistling accent wherein they place great elegance." They also had a reasonably accurate calendar in which a month consisted of three weeks of ten days each.

Endless wars of succession and the meddling of the Portuguese eventually destroyed the Mutapa state. By the nineteenth century the Mutapas ruled only the Zambezi Valley, which offered them little wealth. The last puppet Mutapa was deposed in 1917 by the Portuguese colonizers of Mozambique.

The Torwa State, about 1450–1683

As the Zimbabwe state was declining, a new culture began to grow up on its western fringe. The ruler, who was known as the Torwa, began to build his own *zimbabwe* at Khami in the early fifteenth century. Very little is known about this state, but it was thought to have been very rich because of its close proximity to the gold mines that had once supplied Great Zimbabwe.

In 1683 a ruler of another dynasty, the Changamire, took over the Torwa state and set up his capital at Danangombe (now called Dhlodhlo). In emphasizing their own conquest, Changamire traditional historians tell of how there were two Torwa rulers, Chihunduru and Tumbare. One of them was a powerful magician with either a supernatural horn or an oxtail with which he summoned a cloud of bees to chase away invaders. The Changamire outwitted the rulers by offering them wives who later betrayed their magic secrets to him.

The Changamire State, 1683–about 1840

The Changamire state was said to have been founded by a man called Dombolakonachingwango, or Dombo, for short, who had been a herdsman for one of the Mutapas. Traditions describe him as a very charismatic man who was born to a virgin and became famous as a child who needed only to eat the seeds out of the ground to gain the sustenance of the grown crop. Later, it became clear that Dombo's father was Mwari, the god of all things, who called him to lead the people. He used his powerful personality and the herds in his care to attract followers and seize a portion of the Mutapa's land. Dombo's warriors became known as the Rozvi, which probably comes from the Shona verb *kurozva*, meaning "to destroy." They had a reputation for being very fierce, and it was they who drove the Portuguese from the plateau after the Europeans had been operating forts and trading posts there for almost two hundred years.

The Changamire state was probably the poorest of all the Shona states. Its wealth was based on its cattle, but its power was based on its army, which ranged over a wide area of the plateau. Even though its capital was near the old gold fields of the southwest, by the eighteenth century those fields were almost worked out in terms of the technology available to the Shona at that time. The Rozvi army, however, was the most powerful in southern Africa up until the *mfecane*— or "crushing"—when the Zulu king Shaka rewrote the rules of African warfare and unleashed a tidal wave of violence on the region. (For more on these wars, see *The Land and People of South Africa*.)

The fall of the Changamire state came with the arrival of Ngoni, Nguni, and Ndebele warriors who, fleeing from Shaka, swarmed up from south of the Limpopo. The Rozvi barely weathered the first bands of invaders. The final blow, however, was dealt by a remarkable female

Nguni warrior, Nyamazana, who defeated the Rozvi army and sent the reigning Changamire fleeing from his capital. Somewhere along the way he was killed, leaving the people leaderless. Any hope of ever reestablishing the state ended when the Ndebele under Mzilikazi arrived from the south in about 1838.

Over time, many myths grew up about the Rozvi, adding to their stature among the Shona and with the whites who colonized the country in 1890. Stories abounded of how they moved mountains and built a tower to the moon. They were reputed to have amazing magical powers that came from their special relationship with Mwari. Based on this, many Shona felt that unless a Rozvi was present to confirm the installation of a new chief, it wasn't valid. The Rozvi, who collected fees for this service, did everything to encourage these myths. As recently as the 1960's there were societies in Zimbabwe aimed at reviving the Changamire, but the realities of twentieth-century politics doomed these efforts to failure.

When the white settlers arrived in 1890, none of the great Shona states existed in any way that could seriously challenge them. Most of the Shona people lived under small independent chiefdoms that either paid tribute to the Ndebele in the southwest or lived quietly beyond Ndebele influence. To the British, the Shona were at the very bottom of the heap, conquered both by them and the Ndebele. As such, they treated the Shona with contempt, and over the ninety years of white rule Shona history was all but forgotten. In reality, it is the backdrop against which the much more recent histories of the Ndebele and whites were played out.

Gold mining, about 1890. The Shona shown here are using the same methods they had used for 500 years to obtain the precious metal. National Archives of Zimbabwe

The People
of the Long Shields

The scene that met the king's eyes when the sun rose on that damp, gray dawn in November 1837 was enough to crush even the most valiant spirit. His warriors, feared by every tribe for hundreds of miles, hid like frightened rabbits among the rocks and caves, unwilling, for the first time, to go out and fight. Many, their limbs shattered and their smooth black skin spattered with blood oozing from bullet wounds, would not live to see another dawn. For nine days they had fought, again and again rushing the white men, yelling the blood-curdling cry that had struck terror into the hearts of so many of their enemies. But this time the great ox-hide shields could not protect them. They could not even get close enough to unleash their sharp *assegais* (spears) against their foes. This time their enemies were mounted and had guns, and although they

Chronology

1795   Mzilikazi born

about 1820   Mzilikazi flees Zululand

1825   New Ndebele nation swells to 20,000 people
as result of conquests over Sotho and Tswana
communities north of Vaal River

1829   Mzilikazi meets the missionary Dr. Robert Moffat

about 1833   Lobengula born

1837   Mzilikazi driven out of Transvaal by Boers

about 1838   Ndebele settle in Matabeleland

1854   Moffat visits Mzilikazi, urges him to allow
missionaries, traders, and ivory hunters into
his territory

1868   Mzilikazi dies

1870   Lobengula becomes king

1888   Lobengula signs Rudd Concession

1890   Whites settle Mashonaland

1893   Lobengula and Ndebele defeated by British settler
force

about 1894   Lobengula dies

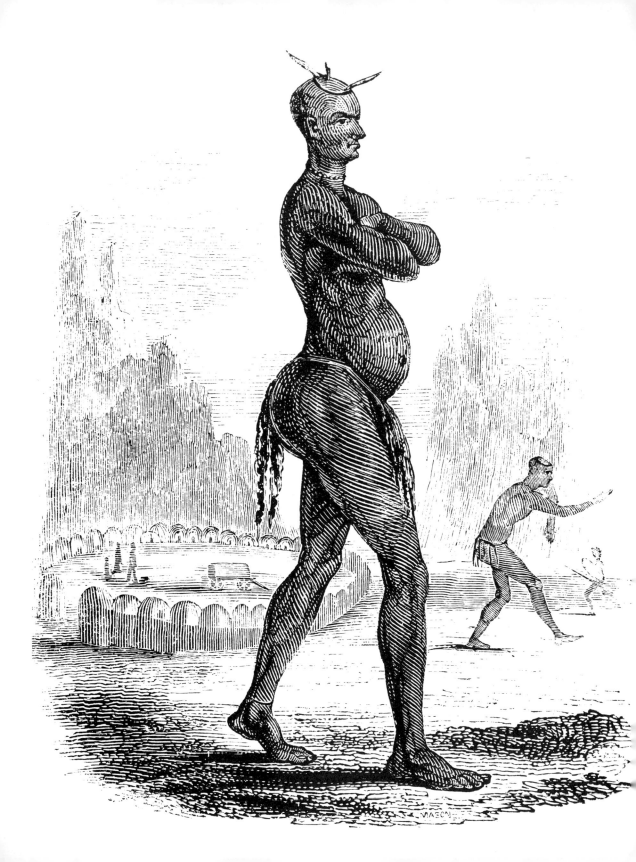

numbered only about one hundred men, they had put to flight an army of ten thousand warriors.

The tale could have ended there and the history of Zimbabwe would have been very different. But it didn't, because this king, Mzilikazi, was a great leader, and in the seventeen years he had searched for a homeland for his new Ndebele nation, he had already overcome enormous obstacles. A vigorous, broad-shouldered man in his forties, Mzilikazi's greatest hour was yet to come. He turned his eyes from the scene of defeat and gathered his counselors around him. Today the Ndebele still speak of this historic moment, for when the *indaba*, or discussion, was over, Mzilikazi pointed northward. "We are going to the great river," he said, "to the *ilizwe ilike Mambo.*" We are going to the country of the Mambo.

The country of the Mambo was, of course, the country of the Shona Changamire. Today, Zimbabwe is still largely the country of the Shona, with the Ndebele comprising only 16 percent of the population. But this proud warrior nation was to play a very important role in Zimbabwe's history, for it was the Ndebele who, at first unwittingly and then unwillingly, gave the British the key that finally unlocked this treasure chest of the African interior to the outside world.

Ndebele Origins

Like many momentous events, the birth of the Ndebele nation in about 1820 began with a seemingly small gesture. Mzilikazi, then an insignificant chief of a small Nguni-speaking clan that lived in what is now the Natal province of South Africa, chopped the plumes off the headdresses of a group of royal messengers who had come to remind him to send a gift of cattle to their king. Such insolence required great daring,

Mzilikazi, father of the Ndebele nation. National Archives of Zimbabwe

· 55 ·

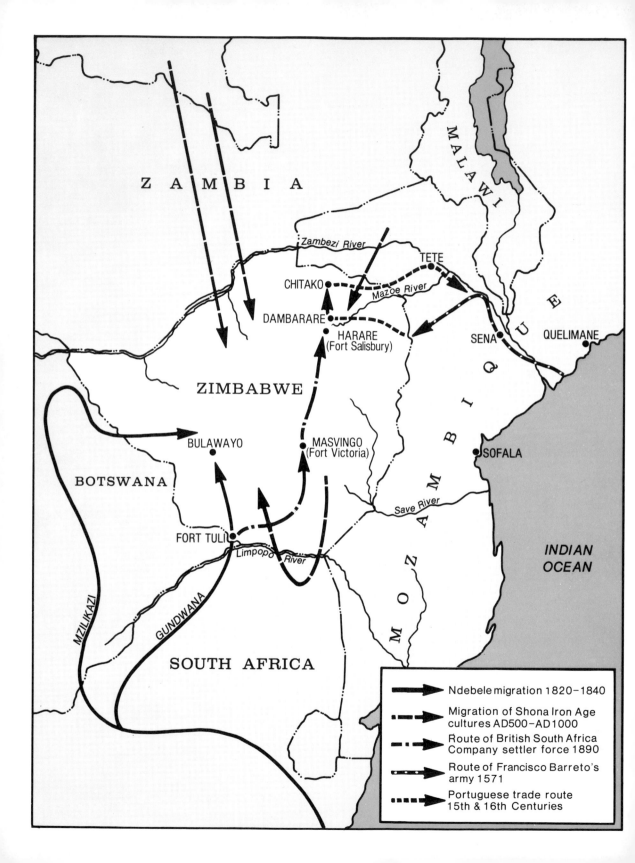

ZAMBIA

MALAWI

Zambezi River

TETE

CHITAKO

Mazoe River

DAMBARARE

HARARE
(Fort Salisbury)

SENA

QUELIMANE

ZIMBABWE

BULAWAYO

MASVINGO
(Fort Victoria)

•SOFALA

BOTSWANA

Save River

FORT TULI

Limpopo River

INDIAN
OCEAN

M O Z A M B I Q U E

MZILIKAZI

GUNDWANA

SOUTH AFRICA

Ndebele migration 1820–1840

Migration of Shona Iron Age
cultures AD500–AD1000

Route of British South Africa
Company settler force 1890

Route of Francisco Barreto's
army 1571

Portuguese trade route
15th & 16th Centuries

because Mzilikazi's king was Shaka, the ruler of the Zulus, who required absolute obedience from all his subjects. Mzilikazi was immediately forced to flee with three hundred followers. It was the beginning of the Ndebele's twenty-year, 1,500-mile (2,400-kilometer) search for a homeland.

No one knows for sure what the word *ndebele* means. For many years it was thought to mean "the people of the long shields," which described the ox-hide shields Ndebele warriors used to protect themselves in battle. More recently, however, scholars have concluded that *ndebele* probably meant "strangers from the east," and was first used by the Sotho who lived in what is now the Transvaal province of South Africa and who were the first people Mzilikazi encountered.

The Search for a Homeland

For years, Mzilikazi and his warriors roved the country south of the Limpopo, living mostly off the livestock and grain stores of communities they conquered. The numbers of his followers swelled with other groups fleeing Shaka and with captured women and children who, over time, became members of his new nation.

Within five years of leaving Zululand, Mzilikazi's kingdom was already the richest and most powerful on the plateau south of the Limpopo and his followers had grown to number twenty thousand people. It was during this time that Mzilikazi met the missionary Dr. Robert Moffat, who was to become his chief intermediary with the white world and his lifelong friend.

In 1836 Mzilikazi was faced with his first white foes. They were the "Voortrekkers" who trundled into his territory in ox wagons. The Voortrekkers, which means migrating pioneers, were white Afrikaner farmers (Boers) and their families, descended from Dutch and French settlers, who were trying to escape the English administration in Cape

Migrations and Invasions

Ndebele Military Tactics

Mzilikazi adopted many of Shaka's revolutionary military tactics. He abandoned the traditional Bantu idea of mustering fighting men from individual clans under the leadership of their chiefs, and instead gathered his warriors into permanent regiments under his centralized command. The *induna*, or regimental commander, was often a man promoted on merit rather than hereditary status. This meant that clan loyalty was replaced by loyalty to the regiment and the king.

The discipline of the Ndebele warriors also set them apart from other Bantu armies. For example, they could run for hours in absolute silence and in perfect formation. They were also encouraged to be as ferocious as possible. One visitor gave this blood-curdling description:

A young bull was turned loose among the soldiers, and the king ordered them to put down their weapons, and without any other help than their hands and teeth, to catch and eat the bull alive. The order was at once obeyed and executed, the young soldiers displaying their fierceness and thirst for blood by at once springing on the animal like

Colony of South Africa and found a nation of their own. Believing theirs was a divine destiny, the Boers were willing to undergo any hardship and face any enemy to fulfill their mission.

In January 1837 a hundred Afrikaner horsemen armed with rifles attacked the Ndebele. It was a wet month. The Ndebele, like most other Bantu, usually fought their wars in the cool, dry winter months between

a pack of wolves, so that in a short time nothing remained except the horns.

Before battle, Mzilikazi would position his regiments in a distinctive formation that resembled the chest, horns, and loins of an ox. Directly facing the enemy soldiers would be the main force or "chest." On either side of the chest would be two flanking "horns." Behind the chest would be a reserve force, the "loins," made up of warriors trained to sit with their backs to the fighting. The main force would engage the enemy in battle while the "horns" ran around and engulfed them from the sides and back. The reserve force would be called upon if needed. The reason they sat with their backs to the fighting was to prevent them from knowing if the battle was not going well for their side.

The Ndebele fought with an *assegai*, a short, broad-bladed spear that was used as an underhand thrusting weapon. They also carried two or three throwing spears and a knobkerrie, or club. To protect themselves the Ndebele covered themselves with a huge ox-hide shield that was strong enough to be used as a battering ram. The Ndebele warriors would run toward the enemy in tight formation with their shields held up to form a wall impenetrable to the spears of their enemies.

May and September. When the Boers struck, they took Mzilikazi completely by surprise. By the end of the day over four hundred Ndebele men, women, and children lay dead and thousands of their cattle were captured. After a second attack in November, the king decided to move his people north. They gathered up what was left of their herds, divided into several groups, and crossed the Limpopo River.

Ndebele war dance, painted by artist-prospector Thomas Baines. National Archives of Zimbabwe

The Establishment of Matabeleland

The Ndebele had few problems with the Rozvi warriors, who were already in disarray after having been attacked by successive waves of armies from the south. Once more Mzilikazi incorporated many of the conquered people—this time the Shona—into his nation.

Although the Ndebele planted crops of their own and built their own settled communities, Mzilikazi still sent *impis*—raiding parties—to terrorize outlying Shona villages. Raiding neighboring communities for women and livestock was very common among many Africans of this time. Disease took its toll on the people and cattle herds alike, and the

survival of the group often depended upon these raids. The Shona, who
had built their villages on *kopjes*, were usually quite capable of defend-
ing themselves against the *impis*.

It is impossible to know how many people were killed each year in
the raids or how far Mzilikazi's *impis* ranged. The events of those years
have become obscured by the views of the white colonizers who romanticized the Ndebele, seeing them either as proud warriors, superior to the
"cringing, cowardly" Shona, or as horrible savages who preyed on a
Shona people who were grateful to be "rescued" by the white settlers.
Over the years, white governments consistently overemphasized the
differences between the Ndebele and the Shona in the interests of
"divide and rule." Intermarriage between the two groups, quite com-

mon at the time the first white settlers arrived in 1890, became much less frequent as the twentieth century progressed and the Shona and Ndebele accepted the white view of their relationship to each other.

The Arrival of the Europeans

In 1854 Mzilikazi's old friend Robert Moffat visited him, and the two took a long wagon journey together. Moffat told Mzilikazi of the great hunger for ivory that existed among white men and that hunters and traders were clamoring to enter the rich, untapped territory controlled by the king. Seeing an opportunity to increase his wealth, Mzilikazi allowed small numbers of Europeans to hunt and trade in the area he controlled. One of them, Henry Hartley, was shooting elephant in what had become known as Mashonaland when he found a reef of quartz that showed visible gold. Nearby were the remains of an ancient mine.

Immediately, all those tales of gold beyond the dreams of avarice once more surfaced to whet the appetites of white adventurers. Like the Portuguese before them, those who saw the mines of the ancient Shona grossly exaggerated their splendor. No matter how much gold was really there, in the capitals of Europe and from just south of the Limpopo the eyes of the whites were now fixed hungrily on this land.

Mzilikazi himself was not to see the consequences.

Lobengula

The coronation of Mzilikazi's son, Lobengula, was a huge affair that involved the blessing of Shona Mwari priests. Over the years the number of Shona incorporated by the Ndebele had grown, until they formed

Dr. Robert Moffat, the missionary who became Mzilikazi's closest friend. National Archives of Zimbabwe

SOUTH AFRICA.
R. MOFFAT.

SOUTHERN DESERT

BAROLONGS

GREAT
NAMAQUALAND

Kuruman

BECHUA

Orange R

GriquaTn

CORANNAS

LITTLE
NAMAQUALAND

BUSHMEN COUNTRY

BASUTOS

CLAN WILLIAM

TAMBOOKIES

Port Nat

WORCESTER

ALBANY

Cape
Good Hope

Algoa Bay

Mzilikazi

*The king is the center and soul of everything. . . . His subjects think
they are made or "grow" only to eat, drink (I wish I could add dress)
and live for Moselkatse. . . .*

Such was Mzilikazi's power over the Ndebele, according to the
missionary Dr. Robert Moffat, who was Mzilikazi's closest friend for
over forty years. That such a friendship could endure so long
between a devout Christian and the man who laid waste a large part
of southern Africa was due in no small measure to Mzilikazi's
charisma.

To those who never met him, the Ndebele King was little more
than a cruel tyrant who ruled his people harshly and showed no
mercy to his enemies. Yet upon personally encountering the King,
most found themselves falling under his spell. Dr. Moffat described
him as having "a pleasing countenance" and being "affable in his
manners." Another missionary, the Rev. Thomas Morgan Thomas,
who had recently lost his wife, was astounded when this "savage"
was moved to tears by Thomas's children. "Take the poor
motherless ones to the wagon, for I cannot bear the sight,"
Mzilikazi cried.

But despite this, Mzilikazi was a brilliant and ruthless military
commander. He was a product of one of the most turbulent periods
in African history, a period when only the strongest survived. This
was something that Mzilikazi himself understood. "I was like a

blind man feeling my way with a stick," he remembered in later years. "We had heard tales of great armies that suddenly popped up from underground or swept down on you from high mountains . . . I had to keep open country around me."

Mzilikazi was clearly a man with exceptional leadership skills. He elicited slavish admiration and loyalty not only from his followers, but also from those he conquered and took into his new nation. Sotho, Tswana, and Shona all became Ndebele. Mzilikazi left Zululand with just 300 followers. By the time he died in 1868, the Ndebele numbered 150,000.

Mzilikazi in his forties was described as being of medium height with a tendency toward overweight. He had simple tastes, preferring to dress like his subjects in the round Zulu headring worn by all adult males and an *um'nwato*, or hollow cone, covering his genitals. He seldom wore jewelry, and his body was scarred from the many battles in which he had fought.

In his last years, Mzilikazi began to suffer from gout and dropsy (both probably consequences of his heavy beer consumption). In 1854, when the King was about sixty, Moffat was shocked to find "the vigorous, active, nimble monarch . . . was now aged, sitting on a skin, with feet lame, unable to walk or even to stand."

The Ndebele never saw him as anything but a mighty leader. At Mzilikazi's death, when he was nearly eighty years old, the message "the mountain has fallen" was relayed throughout his kingdom. Even today the Ndebele speak of the moment of his death with awe: "The lightning flashed out of a clear sky and twelve people fell dead."

the biggest portion of the nation. For Lobengula to take over his father's role not only as King but also as spiritual leader of the nation, it was important that the Shona rites that had become part of the Ndebele religion also be observed.

Immediately, he had to turn his attention to the growing number of whites who were pressing him for permission to preach Christianity, hunt animals, trade ivory, and mine gold in Matabeleland and farther north in Mashonaland. From the start, the history of relations between Zimbabwe's black and white peoples is one of misunderstanding, caused partly by the clash of their vastly different cultures and partly by the inability of the Europeans to take into account the rights and feelings of the Africans. To the whites of nineteenth-century Victorian England, the Africans were a backward race, steeped in ignorance, superstition, and savagery. To the Africans, the whites soon became known as tricksters, rapacious in their greed for gold and land. Perhaps it was a grim omen, therefore, that these two races, who were about to embark together on a rocky ninety-year nation-building adventure, began it at Lobengula's royal *kraal* at Bulawayo, which means "the place of killing."

The Rudd Concession

The success of the British in beating the Germans, Portuguese, and Afrikaners to take control of what was soon to become another corner of the British Empire rests largely on the shoulders of one man: Cecil Rhodes, who was to give his name to the new colony of Rhodesia. Rhodes was an Englishman who had made a fortune in the diamond mines of South Africa and who had grand dreams of extending the

Lobengula, the last king of the Ndebele. There are no photographs of Lobengula because he was very reluctant to have his picture taken. National Archives of Zimbabwe

British Empire "from Cape to Cairo," that is, from the southernmost tip of Africa to the northernmost tip. Standing in that northward path was Lobengula's kingdom, so far unclaimed by any European power and believed to hold unimagined riches. Rhodes set out in his customary single-minded fashion to make sure Matabeleland and Mashonaland would be British, and its riches his.

In 1888 Rhodes sent his business partner, Charles Rudd, to Bulawayo together with Rochfort Maguire, a lawyer, and "Matabele" Thompson, who was renowned for his knowledge of the Ndebele. Lobengula's *kraal* was swarming with white concession seekers, and he kept Rudd and his party waiting endlessly. The whole enterprise almost ended horribly when Maguire was accused of bewitching the river with his red tooth powder. Sir Sydney Shippard, who administered the new British protectorate of Bechuanaland, was sent with an escort of sixteen troopers to help Rudd's case, but he was stopped on the way by an Ndebele patrol convinced that he, too, was a wizard. Later the Ndebele spy who had watched Shippard explained that the white *induna* "took off all his clothes and sat in a pool of boiling water. He rubbed his body all over with a terrible white frothing medicine and squeezed the boiling water over himself with some strange vegetable. Without a doubt he is a powerful wizard."

Eventually, however, Shippard was allowed to enter Lobengula's *kraal.* The outcome was the famous—or infamous—Rudd Concession: Rudd persuaded Lobengula in October 1888 to put his mark to an agreement that granted Rhodes's group exclusive mineral rights in Matabeleland and Mashonaland "together with the full power to do all things that they may deem necessary to win and procure the same." In exchange, they promised to pay the King 1,000 Martini-Henry breech-loading rifles, 100,000 rounds of ammunition, a gunboat to sail on the Zambezi River or £500, and a monthly rent of £100.

The Rudd Concession was the legal piece of paper Rhodes needed to petition Queen Victoria for a charter to colonize Matabeleland and Mashonaland. Within two years Lobengula was presented with the charter, granted to the newly formed British South Africa Company, entitling it to exercise sovereign power in the King's territory.

In June 1890 a "Pioneer Column" of two hundred white settlers accompanied by five hundred company police rolled into Matabeleland in ox wagons. Lobengula had been told this was a working party "going to Mashonaland along the road already arranged with the King." In reality, each settler had been promised fifteen gold claims and a three-thousand-acre farm.

Charles Rudd, who negotiated the infamous Rudd Concession under which Lobengula signed away the mineral rights of his kingdom. National Archives of Zimbabwe

Cecil John Rhodes

Cecil John Rhodes was known as the Colossus of Africa, and indeed, there was nothing small about him: His talents and dreams were as big as his flaws. To him there was nothing so good as an English gentleman, and in his opinion the noblest pursuit any man could follow was to extend the British Empire around the globe.

"We happen to be the best people in the world," Rhodes once declared, "with the highest ideals of decency and justice and liberty and peace, and the more of the world we inhabit, the better it is for humanity." He was ruthless in his pursuit of that ideal, believing that the end justified the means.

Born in Bishop Stortford, England, in 1853, Rhodes was sent, at the age of sixteen, to join his older brother, Herbert, in South Africa, where the climate was thought to be better for young Cecil's chronic asthma. By the time he was thirty-five he was a millionaire, having made a fortune at South Africa's diamond fields in Kimberley. The day came when he bought out everyone mining there with a larger personal check than had ever before been written: "Five Million, Three Hundred and Thirty-Eight Thousand, Six Hundred and Fifty-Eight Pounds—Only."

Rhodes truly believed the extension of British influence in Africa would be good for the Africans, and often declared, "Equal rights for all civilized men south of the Zambezi." Of course, that meant equal rights for all white gentlemen, at least until the Africans could be schooled up to this exacting level of "civilization."

By the time the white settlers colonized Mashonaland in 1890, Rhodes's accomplishments were impressive. Not only had he founded the De Beers Company and Consolidated Gold Fields, two

Cecil Rhodes, founder of the colony of Rhodesia.   National Archives of Zimbabwe

corporate giants that exist to this day, he was also Prime Minister of South Africa's Cape Colony and managing director of the British South Africa Company. He was only thirty-seven years old.

Rhodes could be enormously self-centered and deceitful, yet when he chose, he could show great empathy toward other people, black or white. One early white Rhodesian settler, Miss Rose Blennerhassett, tells of a visit by Rhodes to Umtali (now Mutare) in 1891: "He was besieged with petitions of all sorts. Malcontents and chronic grumblers went to his hut and came away in a few moments cheerful and satisfied . . . the man's mere personal magnetism wrought the change . . . everything about the man is big—faults, virtues, projects. . . ."

The Matabele War

For the next three years the King managed to postpone his downfall, but in 1893 the settlers found an excuse to start a full-scale war with the Ndebele after a feud broke out between a Shona chief and an Ndebele *induna*. Lobengula did not want the war, but the settlers were determined to destroy the Ndebele state.

It was all over within a matter of months. The whites' firepower was so superior that, as in that other fight between Mzilikazi and the Boers over fifty years before, Lobengula's men never came close enough to the enemy to use their *assegais*. With the remnants of his army, the King fled.

The war all but over, the Ndebele did get one last chance to draw some white blood. A small settler force under Major Allan Wilson was sent across the Shangani River to find which way Lobengula had gone,

Rhodes died of heart disease in 1902 in Cape Town. According to his wishes, his body was taken back to the Matopo Hills, where he was interred in a grave cut into a great granite *dwala*. The boulder-strewn brow of this hill commands a superb view of the surrounding countryside. The whites call it World's View, the Ndebele Malindidzimu, which means "dwelling place of the spirits."

Rhodes is remembered today for the Rhodes Scholarships he provided for in his will. These scholarships were to "take the best men for the world's fight" from the English-speaking countries of the world, and send them to Oxford University, his alma mater, where they were supposedly made into gentlemen. Happily, today the scholarships' trustees see fit to award them to women as well.

and discovered he was only about a day ahead. They were told to return immediately, but Wilson disobeyed his orders and pursued the King. It was the rainy season, and Wilson's group was cut off from the main body of the British force by the river's rising waters. The Ndebele attacked and killed every one of the thirty-six men in the group. According to the story that became a symbol of inspiration to succeeding generations of white Rhodesians, the last survivors went to their deaths, hats off, singing "God Save the Queen." Later whites felt that they, too, were holding the standard for civilization in the face of enormous and savage odds.

No one knows for sure what the fate of Lobengula was. He died soon afterward somewhere in the bush. Some say he poisoned himself, others that he died of smallpox. It would be eighty-seven years before another black-ruled state existed in Zimbabwe.

The White Settlers

The two hundred men who made up the settler portion of the "Pioneer Column," as it was always referred to by Rhodesia's whites, were a mixture of South Africans, Englishmen, Canadians, Australians, and Americans. They were mostly between twenty-five and thirty years old, and they came from a wide variety of trades and backgrounds. The sons of English lords rode alongside stonemasons, carpenters, and even a Texas cowpuncher.

Each was chosen to perform a specific task when they arrived at their destination. Some were to create farms, others were to be shopkeepers, still others miners. They gathered in July 1890 at Fort Tuli in what was to become the far southwestern corner of Rhodesia. The "pioneers," like the five hundred BSA (British South Africa) police, were clad in uniform, giving the whole expedition a military air. Their guide was the hunter Frederick Courteney Selous, who was one of the few white men who had traveled extensively in Mashonaland, their ultimate destination.

Fearful of being overwhelmed by hostile Ndebele warriors, the column—ox-drawn wagons and horsemen—followed a route that took them as far from Bulawayo as possible. Selous rode ahead, marking the trees to be cut. He was followed by the road-making crew, of which every second man carried an ax and cut down trees, while the rest held the horses and kept a lookout. Every half hour they changed, the horse holders becoming the tree fellers.

It took four months of incredible effort for the 700 men to travel the 400 miles (680 kilometers) to the small hill they christened Fort Salisbury on September 12, 1890.

White settlers cross a river, from a drawing by Thomas Baines. National Archives of Zimbabwe

Lobengula

"Did you ever see a chameleon catch a fly?" Lobengula once asked a missionary. "The chameleon gets behind the fly and remains motionless for some time, then he advances very slowly and gently, first putting forward one leg and then another. At last, when well within reach, he darts his tongue and the fly disappears. England is the chameleon and I am that fly."

Such was Lobengula's fate, but perhaps the real tragedy is that this King, a barbarian in European eyes, was nevertheless shrewd enough to perceive his own doom. The world into which he was born was on a collision course with a future with which Lobengula was forced to deal every day of his unhappy twenty-three-year reign. That he put off the inevitable as long as he did is a testament to his intelligence and diplomacy.

Born in the early 1830's to one of Mzilikazi's lesser wives, Lobengula was never marked for kingship. When Mzilikazi died, he left no recognizable successor, and the Ndebele split up into factions supporting various claimants to the throne. After some deft political maneuvering, Lobengula was proclaimed King, but it took him two years and a bloody battle to bring the rebellious factions into line. Once the fight was over, Lobengula displayed one of his most remarkable characteristics: an ability to forgive his enemies, even those who had tried to kill him. "If I fight with a person and conquer him it is finished. I don't want to fight him again,"

Lobengula said. No action was taken against the survivors of the rebel groups.

Despite his shaky start, Lobengula eventually inspired great loyalty among the Ndebele. By all accounts, he looked every inch a king. He was over six feet tall, "coppery-bronze in color," and weighed over three hundred pounds, although "not unwieldy in his stoutness."

"Lo Bengula walks quite erect, with his head thrown back and his broad chest expanded," one British colonial administrator reported. "As he marches along at a slow pace with his long staff in his right hand, while all the men around shout his praises, he looks his part to perfection."

In many ways, Lobengula was a great leader, but his talents were different from his father's. He showed adroit political skill in dealing with those in his inner council who disagreed with his conciliatory policy toward the whites. Unlike Mzilikazi, he disliked war and would do almost anything to avoid it.

Lobengula was a vain man and had a weakness for certain aspects of the European culture. For a period when he was young, he dressed in European clothes. As he grew stouter, however, he reverted to the more comfortable traditional Ndebele dress. One settler described him as "a grand old savage," naked "save for a thin roll of blue cloth around his waist," and a skirt of monkey skins.

Lobengula's end was as sad as any deposed monarch's in any other time or place. He was hounded to death.

The Horse and Its Rider

Just seven years after the first white settlers had raised the Union Jack at Fort Salisbury in September 1890, this latest outpost of the British Empire was a bustling frontier town. One hundred fifty miles (255 kilometers) south of the Zambezi, a scattering of low brick buildings with corrugated iron roofs had grown up beneath a *kopje* on the Makabusi River. Already a raw sort of gentility had set in. Ladies, skirts delicately raised, picked their way along muddy streets, averting their eyes from the motley assortment of bearded prospectors, hunters, and scantily clad "natives" who thronged the avenues wide enough for a wagon and sixteen oxen to turn around in. Gentlemen, respectably buttoned into their jackets despite the summer heat, rode bicycles to their jobs as administrators for the British South Africa Company.

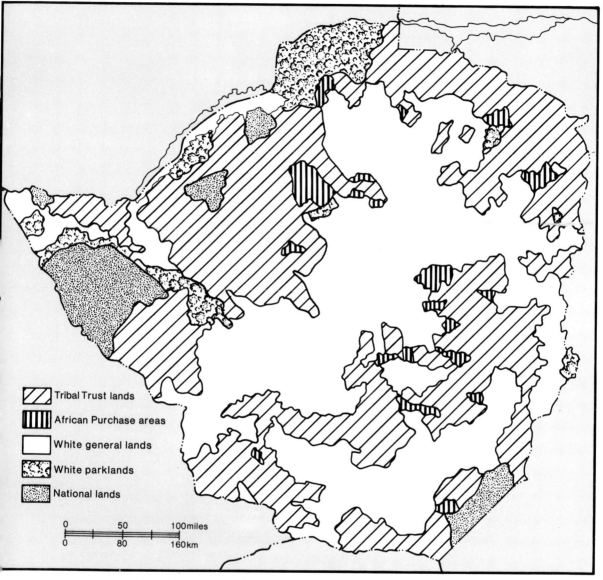

The Division of Land Between Blacks and Whites Before 1979

Tribal Trust lands

African Purchase areas

White general lands

White parklands

National lands

0   50   100 miles
0   80   160 km

Chronology

1890	White settlers occupy Mashonaland
1893–1894	Ndebele War
1894	First Native Reserves set up
1895	Territory proclaimed "Rhodesia"
1896–1897	Ndebele and Shona rebel against white settler occupation
1898	Constitution sets up settler government and franchise for all literate men who can pass strict property qualification
1923	BSA Company rule ends; Southern Rhodesia becomes British Crown Colony
1930	Land Apportionment Act passed, separating country into "white" and "black" areas of occupation
1933	Godfrey Huggins becomes Prime Minister

The social center of Salisbury's "polite" society was Government House, where Rhodesia's second Administrator, Lord Grey, lived with his wife and daughter. Here the white settlers danced to the BSA Police Band. It wasn't quite like home, of course: The ladies often had to ride to the ball on bicycles, pinning their gowns up and putting their fans and gloves in handlebar baskets, and one was as likely to find oneself dancing with a barber as with a baronet.

1939–1945	White and black Rhodesians fight along with Britain in World War II
1953	Federation of Rhodesia and Nyasaland created; Huggins becomes Federal Prime Minister; Garfield Todd becomes Prime Minister of Southern Rhodesia
1959	Government under Prime Minister Edgar Whitehead enacts Law and Order (Maintenance) Act and Emergency Powers Act to quell black political activity
1960	Eleven Africans killed by police, first deaths in independence struggle since 1896 rebellions
1962	Rhodesian Front (RF) formed, wins general election; Winston Field becomes Prime Minister; Nyasaland secedes from Federation
1963	Federation breaks up when Northern Rhodesia secedes
1964	Ian Smith becomes Prime Minister

When not partying at Government House, Salisbury's respectable citizens were shopping at Meikles, the new general store, meeting at the Kettledrum in Pioneer Street for tea and cakes, and putting on amateur plays at the Musical and Drama Society. The weekends were taken up with sports, and there was even a Salisbury Hunt Club that chased jackals and antelope rather than foxes. Almost any white person who behaved in a respectable manner was included, and no one looked too closely at the credentials of some of Salisbury's "aristocracy." There was a "Deacon of Hong Kong," a Lord George Deerhurst who ran the local butcher's shop, and a Vicomte de la Panouse, known as the Count, who had a Cockney wife named Bill. Eccentrics abounded. When local residents Lord and Lady Henry Paulet were married in Cape Town, the best man was a dog named Paddy.

In the summer of 1897 Salisbury's one thousand white inhabitants, like all good British subjects the world over, were celebrating the Jubilee marking Queen Victoria's sixty years on the throne. But beneath the veneer of confidence, more pressing concerns were on their minds. Just the year before, the Ndebele and then the Shona had risen up and rebelled against the yoke the whites had imposed upon them. Hundreds of white men, women, and children had been killed, and the reality of their situation had been brought home to the survivors in chilling clarity: They were very few, surrounded by very many. It was a fear that was to lie at the heart of white Rhodesia until its downfall eighty-four years later.

The First *Chimurenga*

After the defeat of Lobengula in 1893, the British South Africa Company began to carve up the land. Reserves, often in the least desirable locations, were set aside for the Africans who were removed from land sold to white settlers. The company also took Lobengula's cattle as war loot. Unfortunately, the white officials did not understand that there was no clear-cut difference between the King's cattle and the people's cattle, and some of it was held in trust for various ancestors. Among the Ndebele, the King, an ancestral spirit, a married woman, an *induna*, and the man who milked the cow might all have said quite truthfully: "This is my cow." As a result, some Ndebele lost all their cattle, which was not merely their wealth but their tie to their past and their people, as well as their means for marriage and self-improvement. Others had to give up some of their herds as part of a "hut tax" levied by the company.

The British South Africa Company also required both the Ndebele and the Shona to provide young men to work in the mines and on white farms. When there weren't enough "volunteers," newly recruited black policemen were dispatched to get the necessary labor, often employing the *sjambok*, a hide whip, to help prospective workers to make up their minds. The Africans suddenly found their lives controlled by a slew of administrators, magistrates, and native commissioners. Drought and swarms of locusts caused the failure of crops for several years running, and thousands of cattle were killed by rinderpest, a deadly and highly contagious livestock virus.

In late March 1896 the Ndebele rose in what they called *isi ndunduma*—the uprising. It was not a planned rebellion. Instead, spontaneous acts of violence followed one on top of the other. First a black policeman was killed, then a white miner; wagons were attacked, families on lonely homesteads murdered. Selous gave an account of how he and his fellow settlers felt:

For breaking out into rebellion against the white man's rule, I should have borne them no great animosity. . . . I should of course have lent the services of my rifle to help quell the rebellion; but had it not been accompanied by the cruel murders of white women and children, I should not have been animated by the same vengeful feelings as now possessed me, as well as every other white man in Matabeleland. . . .

One white woman gave this description of how merciless some colonists could be: "His shooting of rebel and also loyal natives was horrible to behold. With his revolver he shot one old man sitting on an antheap.

Zhanta, a Shona chief who was one of the leaders of the 1896–1897 rebellion. National Archives of Zimbabwe

We knew this old grey headed man, Gwegula, quite well. He used to walk about with a long staff scaring the birds from our lands. . . ."

Soon the whites had fled to fortified camps in Bulawayo and Gwelo (now renamed Gweru). They were saved by a force of 150 white volunteers from Salisbury, which cornered the Ndebele in the Matopo Hills. In a gamble that won him the name *uMlamlankunzi*—separator of bulls—Rhodes ventured, unarmed, into the Ndebele stronghold and persuaded them to accept peace.

But the settlers' problems were not over. To their horror, in June the Shona had risen in what is now called the first *chimurenga*, or struggle. The Shona revolt followed the same pattern as that of the Ndebele. Lonely farms and mines were attacked, the occupants killed. The whites were appalled. Not only did they consider the Shona timid and cowardly people, they also saw themselves as having "saved" the Shona from the aggression of the Ndebele. In fact, the Shona had suffered the same outrages as the Ndebele. As one white missionary reported at the time, some European farmers and miners had "given the [Shona] a very poor opinion of civilized justice and propriety."

The Shona rebellion proved difficult to suppress. Unlike the Ndebele, who had a tradition of unity, the various Shona chiefdoms rose separately and had to be defeated one by one. Some chiefs remained neutral and others even sided with the settlers. Long accustomed to escaping Ndebele raiders by hiding in the caves and *kopjes* that dotted the countryside, the Shona adopted the same tactics with the settlers. In the end, the whites either starved them out by burning their food stores and fields of grain or blasted them out with dynamite. Shona journalist Lawrence Vambe wrote eighty years later:

The dynamite, or daramete, as the Shona came to call this fiendish white invention, split and blew the rocks into thousands of pieces which became quite as lethal as the white man's bullets themselves. In this way, thousands of Shona

The spirit medium Kaguvi in captivity.
He brought news of the Ndebele
rebellion back to Mashonaland.
National Archives of Zimbabwe

men, women and children were killed, wounded and maimed. . . . As the historians . . . recalled, the countryside echoed with the booms of the guns, big and small, the screams of the fleeing and the dying and for many days, nights, weeks and months, rotting bodies lay strewn everywhere for the vultures and jackals of the Rhodesian bush to feed on.

When it was over, the white authorities looked for the ringleaders. Because in some areas the powerful Kaguvi and Nehanda mediums, in contact with Mkwati, a priest of the Mwari cave cult in the Matopo, were very influential, the belief arose among the whites that the rebellion was inspired by Shona "witches" and "wizards." The two mediums were brought to Salisbury, where they were publicly hanged. Today both are seen as martyrs to the cause of black freedom.

White Domination

Ten percent of the settlers died in the uprisings. Those who survived were a tough and determined lot. They soon discovered there were no easy fortunes to be made in the Rhodesian bush. Bare livelihoods had to be hacked out on lonely farms and mines.

To the settlers' minds, they ruled the country by right of conquest. They were the masters, the Africans their servants. This does not mean that all whites were cruel and unjust. Most thought of the blacks as being like children and the whites as their strict but kindly parents. They saw themselves as the instruments of some higher purpose to spread order and enlightenment. It was one's duty, the white settler thought, to teach the Africans Christian values, encourage them to overcome their "natural idleness," and instruct them in the ways of "progress." Before long, colonial wives were swapping stories of how hopelessly backward their "houseboys" were, while their husbands advised each other on how to discipline a servant who had been "cheeky."

White settlers take Shona crops to try to starve rebels into submission.   National Archives of Zimbabwe

To ensure a regular labor supply, the colonizers looked for ways to make Africans need money so that they would have to work for white pay. They decided to tax the black men. If a man could not or would not pay his full amount in cash, the police would take his cattle and burn his crops and *kraal.*

By 1922 a system had evolved whereby the black women and children stayed at the *kraal*, living on grain and vegetables they grew, while many men lived in the towns where most whites lived. Africans in "white" areas had to register for passes that allowed them to travel to their jobs from "locations"—later, "townships"—where they rented huts. Domestic servants lived on their employers' properties in one- or two-roomed houses called *kias.* No matter what the age of the African male, he was known as the "house boy" or "garden boy." Likewise, to the day she died, a black woman was called "girl." The white employer and his wife were "Boss" and "Madam" to their servants. Domestics were given a very low cash wage because they were fed, clothed, and housed by their employers, who felt they were doing more than enough to take care of their servants' living needs.

In the country, black Rhodesians found themselves in a variety of situations. Those already in reserves were forced to share their land with those who were "removed" from white areas. Others, whose fami-

An Early White Settler and Her Servant Problems . . .

October 20th, 1907

I'm grieved to say that I must part with Whisky. . . . Last Sunday afternoon we went off for the day on our bicycles. . . . But it threatened to rain, so we rode home for tea to find Whisky entertaining two large and oily lady friends in his kia. He had spread out my best teacloth in honor of the occasion and also borrowed my silver teapot and sugar basin. Our arrival was a painful surprise. The ladies vanished, Sixpence put on a virtuous air and told us Whisky was a "skelem," meaning a bad lot, but that he (Sixpence) was a fine, open-hearted, honest, trustworthy fellow. Anyway, Whisky was taken round the side of the house, and well beaten with a sjambok by the muscular Toby, and the victim's howls, instead of upsetting me, were as music in my ears, so infuriated was I.

Personal Memories—Caroline Katsande

We were very poor. My father had died when I was very young. I was the last born of one brother and three sisters. We had a field, but my mother could not work on the land—she had to earn cash, so she worked for other people, for money. Whenever anyone needed some help, my mother would go and work. She needed money for our school fees. I first started to plough when I was 10 years old. In those days, there was something called "bottleneck screening," which meant that not everyone could be educated. I went to school, but I had little time because I also worked as a nanny for other people. My mother would get up at 3 a.m., cook our breakfast, and then go out to work all day. Tea was only something we had on special occasions, when visitors came with sugar and bread. My clothes were second-hand, passed on to me by relatives who lived nearby. When their children could no longer wear the dresses which had become too small for them, then they were given to me. I used to walk one kilometer each day to primary school run by Methodists. I was bright and did well in grade 7, so my brother paid for me to go to secondary school.

lies had often occupied an area for centuries, suddenly found themselves designated as "squatters" on newly acquired white land. They either had to move or were allowed to stay in exchange for working for the white farmer.

During the first thirty years of colonization, roads and railways were built, coal, copper, chrome, zinc, tungsten, antimony, and asbestos were discovered. A yearning to shake loose from company rule also grew among the white settlers, and in 1922 the British government decided to end the company's hold on the country. The self-governing colony of Southern Rhodesia was born.

In the years that followed, the country's whites set up a system that allowed them to totally dominate their black compatriots and deny them all political power. The 1898 constitution gave all literate males, regardless of color, the right to vote, as long as they lived in a house of a certain value, owned a mining claim, or earned a yearly income of at least £50. This automatically excluded almost all Africans. Education, income, and property requirements became the tool by which succeeding white governments prevented blacks from being able to vote.

In 1933 Godfrey Huggins, a doctor of Scottish birth, became the Prime Minister. To his mind, the relationship between the races should

Sir Charles Coghlan and the first Rhodesian cabinet. National Archives of Zimbabwe

Legal Imposition of White Domination, 1890–1961

1891   The Master and Servants Act: Made it a criminal offense for any servant not to obey a "lawful" order of an employer

1895   BSA Company calls for all Africans to register themselves and obtain passes, which they have to produce when entering "white" towns; special passes required by Africans wanting to be in white areas after dark

1908   Rhodesia's Legislative Council passes ordinance preventing white landowners from allowing black tenants to occupy white land

1930   Land Apportionment Act: Gave whites exclusive use of 50.8 percent of total land area of country; the African

be the same as that "between the horse and its rider," with the white man clearly the one in the saddle. The policies of his government reflected this viewpoint.

The Land Apportionment Act of 1930 had already laid the groundwork for his segregationist policies. It led, within a few years, to overcrowding and deterioration in the fertility of the soil. Reclaiming the land they lost became the top priority of black nationalists, and today resettling black families on land that became white owned remains one of the Zimbabwean government's most urgent tasks.

population, 20 times the white population, allocated 29.4 percent

1934	Industrial Conciliation Act: Prevented Africans from qualifying for apprenticeships or skilled work, and from joining trade unions
1950	Subversive Activities Act: Permitted government to ban meetings and literature considered a threat to constitutional government
1958	Public Order Act: Gave government power to detain and restrict anyone without charge or trial
1959	Law and Order (Maintenance) Act, Unlawful Organizations Act, Native Affairs Amendment Act, and Preventive Detention Act: Gave government sweeping powers to curb all civil rights of individuals
1961	Constitution passed promising eventual majority rule for Africans but containing mechanisms for white government to postpone it indefinitely

Federation

After World War II, Huggins and his government began to seriously consider forming a union with Northern Rhodesia (now Zambia) and Nyasaland (which was to become Malawi.) Black unrest in the countries to the north, particularly Kenya, suddenly made the idea of forming a federation very appealing to the whites in all three countries. They hoped that together they could resist the rising tide of black independence that was beginning to lap at their borders. Such a white-ruled union, they thought, might also lead to independence from and recognition by Britain.

In 1953 the Federation of Rhodesia and Nyasaland, popularly known as the Central African Federation, was born. At the time there were just 380 Africans eligible to vote in Southern Rhodesia. As an indication of things to come, the first Federal budget took a half-crown (25 cents) tax off a bottle of whisky and added 5 shillings (50 cents) on a bag of corn, the staple food of the African.

The first five years of federation were prosperous, and all seemed to be going well for the whites, particularly those in Southern Rhodesia. In Salisbury, the federal capital, the first skyscrapers were built; around the country wide, straight roads replaced the gravel tracks and tarred strips that had wended their way through the landscape.

But by 1959 storm clouds were gathering. It became clear that the British government, which felt a responsibility to Southern Rhodesia's Africans, was not going to give independence to the white-ruled union. In Northern Rhodesia the whites began to resent the fact that Southern Rhodesia was benefiting the most from the Federation's prosperity. And Nyasaland, so close to colonies on the brink of independence, was a sea of turmoil.

The Wind of Change

Nineteen sixty, the year British Prime Minister Harold Macmillan gave his famous speech predicting that the "wind of change" was sweeping over Africa, was a watershed year for Southern Rhodesia. The country's police, still known as the British South Africa (B.S.A.) Police, killed eleven Africans during rioting in Bulawayo. They were the first such deaths in what was to be a bloody twenty-year black struggle for Zimbabwean independence. The year before, the two-year-old African National Congress (ANC), the first mass black nationalist movement in Southern Rhodesia, had been banned and three hundred Africans detained under severe new laws devised by Prime Minister Edgar Whitehead to crush organized black political activity.

Farther north, the move to independence was gathering speed. Ghana was the first to achieve it, in 1957; Nigeria, Zaire, Cameroun, the Central African Republic, Chad, Mauritania, and Senegal all followed in 1960. South of the Zambezi, Southern Rhodesia's whites watched these developments with deep misgiving. To them black rule meant chaos. In Kenya the Mau Mau rebellion was resulting in appalling bloodshed, and Zaire's independence had been accompanied by fearful violence. Britain, they felt, was determined to abandon the whites after decades of encouraging them to settle in its African colonies.

When a new constitution was passed in 1961 that increased the black franchise but essentially guaranteed white rule for the foreseeable future, rioting broke out in the black townships. Shops, schools, and beer halls were looted and burned down. In the country, white-owned cattle were maimed and attempts were made to sabotage railway lines and destroy white churches and schools. By the time elections were held in December 1962, Southern Rhodesia's whites were looking for diehard leaders who were willing, at any cost, to stop black rule at the Zambezi. They found such leaders in the newly formed right-wing party the Rhodesian Front (RF). Playing on the fears of the whites, the RF, led by Winston Field, promised to keep Southern Rhodesia a "white man's country" even if it had to break with Britain to do it. The party ran an advertisement that showed a photograph of little girls' legs, black and white, walking together. The headline proclaimed: "Rhodesia is not ready for this." White Rhodesia might not have been, but black Rhodesia had reached the point at which change was imperative.

On election day, Southern Rhodesia's white voters swept the RF into power with a decisive majority. For the next three years, under Field,

Black Political Movements

The Ndebele Home Society: The society aimed to restore the monarchy under Nyamanda, Lobengula's heir, and to create a national homeland for the Ndebele.

The Rhodesian Bantu Voters Association (RBVA): Founded in 1923, the RBVA advocated finding friends among the country's whites to further black interests.

Industrial and Commercial Workers Union (ICU): One of the main forerunners of modern Zimbabwean nationalism, the ICU advocated revolutionary ideas such as the formation of a united black front, regardless of ethnic group, and interracial workers' solidarity. It provided a training ground for later political activists.

The Bantu Congress: Founded in 1934, this was the forerunner of Southern Rhodesia's African National Congress. It called for the extension of voting rights and the exemption of educated blacks from discriminatory laws.

The Youth League: Founded in 1955, this was the first effort at forming a mass black movement.

the new government pressed Britain in vain to grant Southern Rhodesia its independence. The British government would not budge unless the Southern Rhodesians agreed to gradually repeal discriminatory laws and widen the franchise until black majority rule was eventually achieved.

The Southern Rhodesian African National Congress (SRANC): The SRANC was formed in 1957. Led by Joshua Nkomo, it was banned under the emergency laws passed in 1959.

The National Democratic Party (NDP): Also under Nkomo's leadership, the NDP was truly a mass movement made up of black students, teachers, shopkeepers, organized labor, farm workers, and peasants. It was the first group to abandon behind-the-scenes agitation in favor of rallies and mass demonstrations.

The Zimbabwe African People's Union (ZAPU): ZAPU took over from the banned NDP. It called for a universal franchise with "one man one vote." Although it was banned in 1962, ZAPU played a major role as the Ndebele people's political and military representative in the liberation struggle. It was formally absorbed into ZANU-PF in 1987.

The Zimbabwe African National Union (ZANU): ZANU was created in 1963 by the Rev. Ndabaningi Sithole after a violent split with ZAPU. Robert Mugabe was a member of ZANU's first executive. It became the Shona voice in the struggle of the 1960's and 1970's. Today ZANU-PF (ZANU-Patriotic Front) is the official party of Zimbabwe.

In 1963 the Federation formally broke up. The next year the new black-ruled states of Zambia and Malawi were born. Dissatisfied with his performance as Prime Minister, the RF removed Field and replaced him with Ian Smith, the man whose tenacity allowed white Rhodesia to survive fifteen more hard-fought years.

A Short Thousand Years

Lunchtime on Thursday, November 11, 1965, could hardly have appeared more normal. The oppressive heat of October had not yet given way to the rainy season, Africans snoozed under trees in Cecil Square in central Salisbury, Union Jacks flapped languidly over government buildings. Yet all around the country, in offices, on the verandas of suburban houses, in farm kitchens, Southern Rhodesia's whites and many of its blacks were gathered around their radios. The voice they listened to was that of Prime Minister Ian Smith. "I believe that we are a courageous people and history has cast us in a heroic role," he said in the flat monotone that would soon become familiar to people around the world.

To us has been given the privilege of being the first Western nation in the last two decades to have the determination and fortitude to say 'So far and no further.' . . . We Rhodesians have rejected the doctrinaire philosophy of appeasement and surrender. . . . We have struck a blow for the preservation of justice, civilization and Christianity. . . .

With these grand words Smith announced that his government had, after seventy-five years, cut all its ties to Britain. It had defiantly made a unilateral declaration of independence, known ever after as UDI. His government, Smith said, would have independence on white Rhodesia's terms, not on Britain's terms, which insisted on eventually turning over the government to Rhodesia's black majority. Although it was never recognized by Britain or the outside world as such, Southern Rhodesia ceased to be a colony that day and became Rhodesia, a nation in rebellion.

Many white Rhodesians, especially those with close ties to England, felt some foreboding about how the country would fare, but the great majority enthusiastically lined up behind Smith. Soon people were refusing to stand when "God Save the Queen" was played, and cars were sporting bumper stickers that read "Forward Rhodesia" and "I hate Harold," referring to British Prime Minister Harold Wilson. Wilson had vowed he would bring Rhodesia to its knees in six weeks with economic sanctions. Smith promised his white compatriots there would never be black rule in Rhodesia in a thousand years. It would take fifteen years and a bloody civil war to end the white rebellion.

Sanctions

By 1968 white Rhodesia found itself in the position of the proverbial mouse that roared. The outside world, reluctant to send military force,

Chronology

1965	November 11: Prime Minister Ian Smith makes unilateral declaration of independence from Britain
1966	United Nations imposes selected sanctions on Rhodesian imports and exports
1968	U.N. imposes mandatory sanctions on all Rhodesian imports and exports
1969	Smith government introduces new constitution calling for total segregation in all spheres of life, holding out promise of eventual parliamentary "parity" for races; passes Land Tenure Act imposing permanent segregation of land occupancy
1970	Rhodesia becomes a republic, not recognized as legal by the outside world
1971	Smith reaches settlement with British government, holding out promise of eventual, but distant, majority

was determined to squeeze the rebel colony into submission by completely isolating it. People holding Rhodesian passports were unwelcome almost everywhere, and the United Nations imposed a total trade embargo on the country. On paper it seemed like a good idea. Rhodesia was a landlocked country, it had no oil of its own, and its economy depended upon its mineral and tobacco exports. It had to import almost

rule for Africans; Bishop Abel Muzorewa forms African National Council (ANC)

1972   Pearce Commission judges black opinion to be against settlement; reinvigorated guerrillas step up activity

1974   African nationalist leaders released from prison, go into exile

1976   Formation of Patriotic Front

1977   Smith seeks settlement with internal African groups

1979   UANC (United African National Council) under Muzorewa wins elections; Muzorewa becomes Prime Minister of Zimbabwe Rhodesia; Land Tenure Act repealed, ending segregation; Lancaster House conference convened in London; British-proposed constitution accepted; ceasefire goes into place

1980   Mugabe's ZANU-PF wins first free election; April 18, Zimbabwe becomes independent state, with Robert Mugabe as first Prime Minister

all manufactured goods, from big items—such as cars, farm and mining machinery, and aircraft—to little things like light bulbs, canned fish, and chocolate. The embargo failed, however, to bring a quick end to the rebellion, mostly because some countries did not join in the sanctions and others kept trading with Rhodesia on the sly.

By imposing the embargo, the United Nations hoped to demoralize

Ian Douglas Smith

"Thus far and no further" was one of Ian Smith's favorite phrases. It embodied not just his view of how much—or how little—black participation he would permit in Rhodesia's affairs, but was also indicative of his most prominent characteristic: an unbending will.

He was born in 1919 near the small mining town Selukwe, which is now known as Shurugwi, the son of an immigrant Scottish butcher and cattle dealer. A farmer by calling, Smith's attitudes were typical of those of many white Rhodesians of his generation. "I cannot see in my lifetime that the Africans will be sufficiently mature and reasonable to take over," he once said. Like Cecil Rhodes, he believed white rule was not just good for whites, but good for Africans, too. He devoted his life to preserving Rhodesian society as it existed before 1980.

Possessing neither speaking talent nor great intellect, Smith seemed an unlikely choice for a leader who commanded loyalty that almost amounted to a cult following among Rhodesia's whites. Many white homes displayed paintings, copper plaques, and posters of the man, and criticism of him was seldom heard. What white Rhodesians saw when they looked at Ian Smith was a man of unyielding principle who was willing to stand firm against the forces of permissiveness, hypocrisy, and double standards that he believed were undermining the West. He was a force that stood between them and communism, Rhodesia's whites believed, personifying the image they had of themselves: honest and forthright, dedicated to preserving civilization, orderly government, and high standards.

Ian Smith autographs photographs of himself, 1978. Times Media Ltd

With "good old Smithy" at the helm, they believed, Rhodesia could withstand whatever the world threw at it.

To the black nationalists, Ian Smith represented only one thing: white oppression. He was a harsh and unbending figure who stood for everything brutal Africans had experienced at the hands of white Rhodesia. To those who tried to negotiate with him, he was cunning and unreliable. "Your reputation as a devious and lying twister is even worse than mine," U.S. Secretary of State Henry Kissinger told him in 1976. "But let me warn you not to try any funny stuff with me because this time you will have met your match."

A fighter pilot in World War II, Smith smashed his face when he crashed his plane in a predawn takeoff. The accident left him with

the white population of Rhodesia. Exactly the opposite happened. The Rhodesians closed ranks and made a game of evading the sanctions and living with the inevitable shortages. Gasoline rationing was instituted, and resourceful businessmen began to manufacture some of the luxury goods that had disappeared from the shelves. Rhodesian-made wine, chocolate, and jam all made their debut, and although they tasted horrible, Rhodesians consumed them in the name of patriotism.

The standard of living for white Rhodesians continued to be high. The average white family could afford to live in a three-bedroom house with a swimming pool and employ two servants who lived in the *kia* in the backyard. Taxes were low; white children received a good education at almost no cost in whites-only schools. With the sunny, pleasant climate it was a life few whites were willing to leave. The Rhodesia they

a slightly crooked nose and an eye that drooped, giving his face a strange, immovable quality that added to his aura of rocklike firmness.

For fifteen years Smith had complete control of the Rhodesian government. His simple, fixed beliefs and unwillingness to compromise were seen as folly by those outsiders who tried to resolve the Rhodesian dispute.

Still convinced of the righteousness of his cause, Smith has been unrelentingly hostile to the current government. He nevertheless remained in politics after 1980, heading the all-white Conservative Alliance of Zimbabwe (CAZ).

Today he can sometimes be seen walking his dog in Belgravia, one of Harare's more expensive suburbs, past the houses of his neighbors, the Cuban and Chinese ambassadors.

knew was one of tidy suburbs and pleasant streets lined with purple-blossomed jacaranda trees, afternoon tea, *braaivleis* (barbecues), and Sunday cricket matches. The only Africans most whites encountered were their servants, lowly government messengers, and the few black tradespeople who plied their wares on the suburban streets. Where these people came from each day and where they went each night was a mystery to most whites. Few had occasion to visit the teeming black townships outside the white cities, and the rural Tribal Trust Lands were usually seen fleetingly through car windows.

The world of the black Rhodesian was quite different. Eighty percent of the women were forced to live in the rural areas because there was little work for them in the cities, and without work they were unable to get passes to be there. In the townships, crime was rife and there was

"Rhodesians Never Die"

(Song by Clem Tholett
Sung by White Rhodesians)

We'll preserve this nation
For our children's children
Once you're Rhodesian no other land will do,
We will stand tall in the sunshine
With truth on our side,
And if we have to go it alone,
We'll go it alone with pride.

We're all Rhodesians
And we'll fight through thick and thin
We'll keep our land a free land
Stop the enemy coming in
We'll keep them north of the Zambezi
Till that river's running dry
And this mighty land will prosper
For Rhodesians never die.

a constant shortage of housing. The noisy, littered, usually untarred, streets were crammed with battered old cars, bicycles, and buses packed to bursting with people, luggage, and household goods wrapped in blankets. People were always on the move, some just arriving from the country to find work, others departing to visit their families or forced to leave because they had lost their jobs.

Suburban matrons while away an afternoon playing lawn bowls, a popular pastime for Rhodesian whites.   Jason Laure

Illegal Republic

By 1969 Rhodesia had become a major embarrassment to Britain. Several rounds of talks had been held during which British resolve rather than Rhodesian resolve was chipped away. The more Harold Wilson was willing to compromise, the more intransigent Ian Smith became. That year Smith introduced a new constitution that made Rhodesia a republic and, in Smith's words, "sounded the death knell of the notion of majority rule." Africans were given sixteen seats in Parliament, whites fifty seats. Provision was made for an increase of black representation, but the rate was so slow that it was estimated it could take 460 years before there was any increase in African seats, and 980 years before there would be equal black and white representation. Smith's government also introduced the new Land Tenure Act, replacing the old Land Apportionment Act. It imposed new restrictions on the black population and divided the country equally into white and black areas, with each race getting 45 million acres (18 million hectares).

The Turning Point

Settlement seemed close in 1971, when Smith signed an agreement with a new British government headed by the Conservative Party. Under the agreement, the principle of majority rule was accepted, but again the pace of evolution to black government was glacially slow. The one sticking point was that the British government insisted black Rhodesians also approve of the plan. A twenty-four-member commission under Lord Pearce was dispatched to the rebel colony to test black opinion. Smith was confident that this was a mere formality. He boasted that Rhodesia had "the happiest Africans in the world."

Horrified at what the settlement meant for black rule in the country, the few nationalists not under detention threw themselves into muster-

"*Chimurenga Song*"

(Sung by Guerrillas)

Hark!
It Thunders!

Smith! Our brothers and sisters
Are living in the forests
Because they are protecting our land
Smith! Our brothers and sisters
Are living in the forests
Because they are fighting for our
country.

They would have wanted
To sleep under a roof
They would have wanted
To till their lands
But for the love of our land
But for the love of our land

They are fighting for our land
They are fighting for our land.

ing black opposition. A little-known United Methodist bishop, Abel Muzorewa, launched the African National Council (ANC) and, within four weeks, had started a groundswell of black discontent and opposition. The arriving commissioners were met by rowdy crowds opposing the settlement, and riots broke out in Salisbury, Umtali (modern-day

Mutare), and Gwelo (Gweru). Five months later, in May 1972, the Pearce Commission delivered its judgment: "In our opinion, the people of Rhodesia as a whole do not regard the proposals as acceptable as a basis for independence." The settlement was dead.

This was a turning point for African nationalism in Rhodesia. For the first time since white colonization, the country's blacks had had a small taste of victory. The passivism of the past was swept away and a new purpose galvanized the nationalist movement.

The Second *Chimurenga*

The guerrilla war that escalated into the bitter civil war of the 1970's actually began in 1964. Small bands of rebels carried out hit-and-run attacks on white farms, but the inexperienced guerrillas were usually caught by the Rhodesian soldiers, and their caches of arms and ammunition discovered.

Nineteen seventy-two marked the real beginning of the second *chimurenga*. ZANU guerrillas, organized into the Zimbabwe African National Liberation Army (ZANLA), began to lay the groundwork for an organized campaign in the mountainous and sparsely inhabited northeast corner of Rhodesia. Quietly, the guerrillas worked at winning the support of the local spirit mediums and reminded the village folk of all their grievances against the whites. By the time they launched their first attacks, ZANLA had recruited hundreds of people to act as porters and guides, and they had hidden weapons—mortars, rocket launchers, land mines, Russian and Chinese-made guns—in dozens of villages around the countryside. Once again isolated white farms were attacked, roads ambushed, and dirt roads land-mined. It was the beginning of a dirty

A rural African listens as members of Britain's Pearce Commission gauge his opinion on the 1972 settlement proposals between Rhodesia and Britain. AP/Wide World Photos

ZANLA guerrillas.   Julie Frederikse

war that brutalized both sides and led to the deaths of almost thirty
thousand people.

Realizing it was now facing an enemy that was operating with the help
of the local people, the government decided the best way to fight the
war was to deny the guerrillas that support. Hefty fines, often taken in
the form of cattle, were imposed on villagers suspected of helping the
guerrillas. Whole villages were made to suffer for the actions of individuals. Those people living along the northeast border were removed
from their homes, and later whole areas were depopulated as peasants
were herded into fenced "protected" villages. The inhabitants were
permitted to leave the villages during the day to tend their gardens, but

they had to be back before a six-P.M. curfew. Those who were not were often shot by trigger-happy guards.

Rhodesia's whites were convinced they were fighting communism, not their compatriots, and with heavy press censorship and complete control of radio and television, Smith was able to keep them in a state of ignorance about the extent of guerrilla infiltration. Only the white farmers, who bore the brunt of the guerrilla attacks, knew how serious the situation was. But with everything staked on their land, they simply adapted to life in the "sharp end," as they called it, and stayed. They installed alarms, sandbagged their homes, and surrounded them with

A black government soldier guards one of the "protected villages" set up to isolate rural peasants from the guerrillas. AP/Wide World Photos

Personal Memories—
Elizabeth Moyo

One night, my mother was called out. We don't knock on doors, we clap. Someone clapped outside my mother's door, calling her to a meeting. . . . A n'anga (diviner) was there and a woman who was a spirit medium. . . . She had come to pass on a message. It came from the spirit medium of Nehanda and it was very important. It told the women they should open their huts to the boys.

At the beginning, nothing happened. The boys who had come in, the vakomana, had crossed the border. They never slept in the village, they just came for food, and no one ever asked them any questions. They were fed, they were there, and then they were gone. . . . One morning, they heard an unusual noise. Later they found out what they were—helicopters. They came in, I don't know where they landed, but they came in. They went through the village like cockroaches . . . no, like locusts. Locusts eat everything that is in their way. And that is what the soldiers did. They went through the village, they pulled

high, electrified security fences. They armor-plated their jeeps and Land Rovers to withstand the blast of land mines. They moved their beds away from windows and slept instead in the interior passages of their houses. They stayed home at night. During the day both the men and women went about their chores with automatic rifles cradled in their elbows.

Many were the accusations from both sides about who committed the ghastly acts of brutality perpetrated on the poor peasants who were

women out of their huts, they made them lie on the floor with hands outstretched. The children, some of whom were tied to their mother's back, were crying, but it made no difference to the soldiers. They pulled my grandmother out of her hut. They threw her pots all over the place, breaking them. Then they took four of the young women and took them away. The villagers could hear their screams. It went on for hours. And then, the next morning, one of the Black soldiers who were with the security forces came in and said, "You can go and get them." They got into their helicopters and went away. The women were dead. They had been tortured. When the Smith forces talk about political consciousness, it's a joke really. How else can you get politically conscious? Unless it's through incidents like this. Some weeks later, the soldiers came back. This time, when the helicopters came, many people ran away and hid in the bush, but the soldiers found them and drove them back to the village. They made them get on to lorries [trucks], told them to pack a few pots and other things. When the villagers asked where they were going, they were not told. But this was one of the first keeps that they were taken to. You know the keeps, the villages that they put up to break contact between the vakomana and the local people. My grandmother spent three years in a keep.

caught between the two forces. The Smith government blamed the "terrorists," while the guerrillas blamed the army, in particular the Selous Scouts, a hardened band of black and white soldiers who specialized in bush warfare. In the cities, newspaper readers were frequently treated to lurid descriptions of atrocities. It stiffened white belief in the justness of their cause.

For the African villagers it was a no-win situation. If they sheltered the guerrillas, they risked punishment from the soldiers. If they refused

Justin Chauke
Remembers Guerrilla Training

One of the things we had learned . . . was how to decide whether water was safe to drink or not, but this became much clearer in practice. . . . First you watched to see if there was life in the pool, fish or any living thing. If there was, it was a good sign that the water was okay. As far as burying arms is concerned, the most important thing is to thoroughly examine the terrain before you decide to bury the arms. If you observe certain features like hills and so on, you'll want to look at your compass so if you send someone who was not present when you cached the arms it won't be too difficult to locate them. Another thing we learned was that when you come to a river, even if you're very thirsty, you don't go straight to the water and drink before crossing the river. Your first task is to cross the river and then drink, because if you get to a river and you all go down and drink, the enemy may have already spotted you and you will all be gunned down with your heads down in the water. So you must cross the river first. Then having ascertained that there is no enemy around, your next task is to drink. You also have to do reconnaissance even when it appears there is no enemy around, before you cross the water or the river, or before you just go to a pool, to make sure you are not found on all fours.

to help the guerrillas, they were accused of collaborating with the government and were killed to deter others thinking of doing the same thing. In one memorable incident in April 1974, the village of Musiwa was destroyed by the government forces, and its 255 inhabitants, of whom 187 were children, were relocated 450 miles away near Beitbridge in a completely alien and unsuitable environment. The reason the government gave was that the village had become a guerrilla base. The headman later admitted they had been helping the guerrillas. "If we had not," he said, "we would have been killed. So what else could we do?"

Although some rural Africans supported the guerrillas because they had no choice, many others did so because they genuinely wanted to be part of the "liberation struggle." For these people, the guerrillas, which included women fighters, were affectionately known as the *vakomana* and *vasikana*, "the boys" and "the girls." An increasing number of young people left Rhodesia to become guerrillas. They were trained in Tanzania, Mozambique, and Zambia before returning to fight.

Negotiations

Between 1972 and 1976 various futile attempts at negotiations took place between Smith and the nationalist leaders. The black nationalist leaders Robert Mugabe, Joshua Nkomo, and Ndabaningi Sithole, who had all been in political detention for ten years, were released from prison in 1974 and were exiled. Both sides felt they could fight on indefinitely, and therefore neither side felt the need to compromise. Nothing less than black majority rule would do for the nationalists, and Smith would not agree to that. "I don't believe in majority rule, black majority rule, ever in Rhodesia," he said, "not in a thousand years."

With each passing year, however, Rhodesia's resources became stretched ever thinner. By 1976 every able-bodied white man under age thirty-eight was being called up periodically to fight. The country's economy began to suffer. Whites began to emigrate in increasing numbers. Grim humor rather than cheerful solidarity became the order of the day. The road that ran south from Salisbury to South Africa ceased to be known as the "chicken run," so named because only cowards

Personal Memories—
Mark Jacobsen

It was bad when we went to the sharp end. Most of us had lived in Salisbury all our lives and suddenly we were tramping around the bush, sweating our guts out, wondering if there was some terr [guerrilla] round the next corner about to blow us away. . . . It was almost a relief when we finally got to shoot at something. . . . That first time, whoever it was shot back a bit and then just disappeared. . . . Our Af [African] tracker followed the footprints right into a kraal and there was all these bloody Afs just sitting around as if butter wouldn't melt in their mouths. . . . We didn't hurt them, but we scared the bejesus out them. Told the headman if he didn't tell us where the terrs had gone we'd shoot his family. He resisted at first, so we took one of his wives round the side of a hut and fired a shot into the air. Told him we'd shot her. We were about to do Wife Number Two when he recovered from his memory lapse. . . .

The worst experience was one night I was out with four other guys. We'd sacked out and left one bloke on watch. I woke up at some point and had to take a leak, so I got up and walked a short distance away from the camp. . . . I was just standing there, looking at the sky, feeling worried because it was so dark and overcast when I heard automatic rifle fire. I dived for cover and just lay there. I knew right away what had happened. Some terrs had fired on the guys. I stayed right where I was until it got light. I didn't even do up my fly. When it was light I crept over to the camp and everyone was dead. Killed right there in their sleeping bags. One bloke looked like he was just asleep, except there was this huge blood stain on his bag.

"I keep my pistol ready," said this elderly woman, who in 1978 was living on a farm near Mutare. The farm, like others in the area, had been subjected to mortar attack from ZANLA guerrillas a stone's throw away in Mozambique. AP/Wide World Photos

supposedly left the country, and was redubbed the "owl run," because emigration was now considered the wise thing to do.

In 1976 U.S. Secretary of State Henry Kissinger persuaded Smith to accept the notion of black majority rule in Rhodesia within two years, but he was unable to broker a settlement that satisfied the nationalists. For some years, ZANU and ZAPU (Zimbabwe African People's Organization) had been at odds and their leaders, ZANU's Mugabe and ZAPU's Nkomo, disliked and distrusted each other. Now sensing victory close at hand, these two old antagonists decided, at least temporarily, to put aside their dislike for each other and form a loose alliance called the Patriotic Front.

The situation in Rhodesia was going downhill fast. Thousands of people were dying each month. Some of them were combatants, but many were African peasants who were caught in the cross fire, stepped on land mines, or were murdered by one side or the other for collaborating with the enemy. Morale among the whites was at an all-time low. All reasonably fit men between the ages of thirty-eight and fifty were now being called up to fight; businesses were going bankrupt because the white employees had to spend so much time doing military service. Doubts about what kind of future they were fighting for increased the mood of despair, and the trickle down the "owl run" became a steady stream.

Smith decided to try negotiating an "internal settlement" with "moderate" black leaders like Bishop Muzorewa, who had built up a large following within Rhodesia. The settlement left whites in control of twenty-eight out of one hundred seats in Parliament, and also allowed them to continue to control the civil service (government bureaucracy), the economy, the police, and the armed forces. The Patriotic Front and the outside world dismissed it as a sham, but elections were nevertheless held in April 1979 in which Bishop Muzorewa emerged the winner. He became the Prime Minister of the new state of Zimbabwe Rhodesia, but it was a hollow victory. The war still raged on.

Lancaster House

In Britain a new conservative government under Prime Minister Margaret Thatcher had just gained power. The time seemed ripe for one last stab at ending the Rhodesian dispute at the negotiating table rather than in a fight to the death.

In September 1979 the British Foreign Secretary, Lord Carrington, brought together Prime Minister Muzorewa's delegation (which included the stubborn Smith) and the Patriotic Front at Lancaster House

Jubilant Mugabe supporters celebrate his election in 1980.   Jason Laure

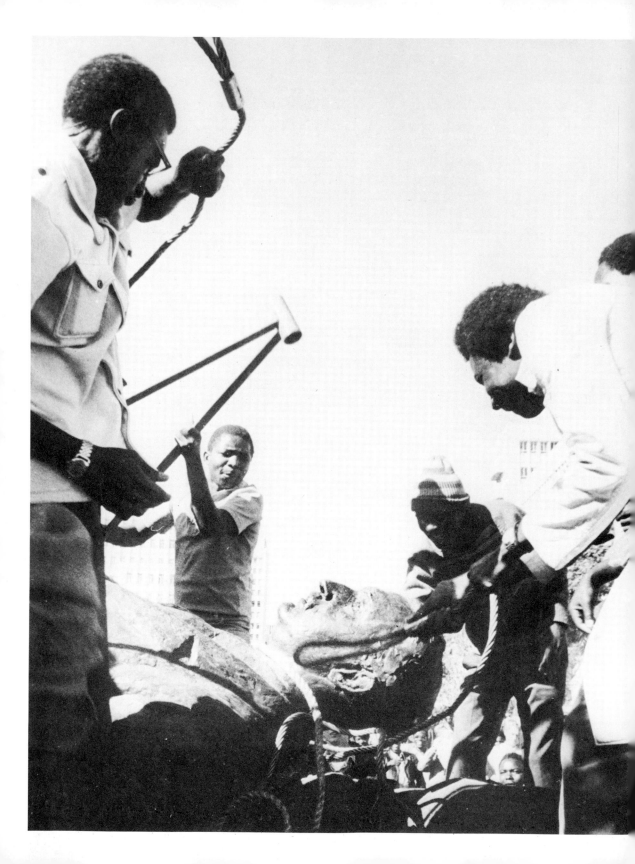

in London. At every turn it appeared as if the talks would break down, but somehow Lord Carrington held them together. Finally, on December 21, after three stormy months at the negotiating table, Muzorewa, Mugabe, Nkomo, and Carrington signed the agreement that ended the seven-year war and heralded the birth of the new, independent state of Zimbabwe.

Between then and the elections in February 1980, the Union Jack once more flew over the legal British colony of Southern Rhodesia. On March 4 it was announced that Robert Mugabe's Shona-dominated party, now called ZANU-PF (ZANU-Patriotic Front), had been swept into power with 63 percent of the vote.

On April 18, 1980, the British flag was hauled down for the last time, almost ninety years after it was first raised. In the renamed capital, Harare, an ecstatic crowd hauled down a statue of Cecil Rhodes that stood on one of the major thoroughfares. White rule was a thing of the past and an independent black state of Zimbabwe was born.

Jubilant blacks celebrate the end of colonialism by flogging the statue of Cecil Rhodes that stood for decades in the heart of the capital. AP/Wide World Photos

The Revolution
Meets Reality

Early each weekday morning Zinyoro Mariga positions himself outside
the gates of one of the many factories located in Bulawayo. Like the
dozens of other young men who are there, he is armed with a long
bamboo stick. There is a lot of good-natured jostling among the men
who see themselves as comrades-in-arms in the eternal battle to find
employment.

Sometimes just before eight A.M. when the workday begins, a factory official comes out to look for short-term labor. Immediately, everyone presses forward to the gates to thrust his identity card through
the bars. Those at the back stick their cards in a cleft in the bamboo
and try to pass them over the heads in front of them. Maybe two or
three of the thirty or forty people will be given work for the day. The

rest sigh and shrug their shoulders. Zinyoro hurries away to fresh
hunting grounds. He has heard that the easiest places to find work
these days are at security firms, which, with the rising crime rate
caused by the high unemployment, are among the fastest growing
businesses in Zimbabwe.

For President Robert Mugabe and the government of Zimbabwe,
people like Zinyoro are no laughing matter. Each year since independence, more and more young people like him have poured out of the
schools into a society that cannot give them jobs. When Mugabe came
into power in 1980, he promised everyone an education, and he has
largely succeeded in carrying out that promise. What he didn't promise,

*Refugees returning to Zimbabwe at the end of the civil war after living in exile in
Mozambique.* United Nations

but what was implied, was that there would be work for all these newly educated people.

The figures are frightening. In December 1988, the end of the Zimbabwean school year, 120,000 students graduated. Only 24,000 found work. In 1992, the first year an entire generation will have made its way through the school system, 330,000 youngsters are expected to graduate. There will be jobs for only 30,000 of them.

It all seems very far from the euphoria most Zimbabweans felt in 1980 at the time of independence. People like Zinyoro have watched the rising black middle class take over the formerly all-white suburbs, acquire expensive cars, and live the life that used to be reserved for whites only. Where, they ask, is the ideal socialist state promised by President Mugabe and the officials of ZANU-PF? Why are there still people who have so much, while others have so little? Mugabe is not deaf to these awkward questions, but he soon discovered that ideology was no match for reality.

In a continent where collapsing economies are the norm rather than the exception, and where starvation and malnutrition take millions of lives each year, Zimbabwe is, despite its problems, still an oasis. It enjoys a shaky economic stability, which the President has sought to maintain while the country goes through the long transition from white-led capitalism to black-led socialism.

Reconciliation

At the time of independence, the late President Samora Machel of Mozambique gave Mugabe this piece of advice: "Don't make my mistakes. Don't attempt radical changes overnight. Keep your economy going above all else. Keep your whites." It is advice Africa's newest

Socialism

The German philosopher Karl Marx was the leading proponent of socialism. All people, not just an elite group of owners, he said, should control the economy of a society and benefit from it. The workers should sweep away the class system, which perpetuates inequality, and seize "the means of production," i.e., the factories and mines and farms. Once this "workers' revolution" has taken place, Marx said, the society can be reordered. No elite would be permitted to control the rest of the people by virtue of their ownership of the economy. Society would distribute the goods produced by the workers equally.

Socialism and its close cousin, communism, are hostile to capitalism, which they see as the basis for the class system. Under capitalism the "means of production" are privately owned and operated for profit. Ideally, they compete with each other without the interference of the government.

Socialism has always been a popular philosophy among oppressed people who have suffered under any unjust system controlled by a minority. It is not surprising, therefore, that many nationalist struggles in colonial Africa were fought under the socialist banner. A just distribution of the country's goods seemed to go along with the just distribution of political power expected at independence. This feeling was bolstered by the fact that many nationalists, including those in Zimbabwe, were supported in their struggles by communist states such as the Soviet Union and China.

leader heeded. He swallowed his pride, overruled ZANU-PF hardliners who wanted to dispossess the whites, and extended the hand of reconciliation to his former enemies. The country's new leader realized Zimbabwe needed its whites, at least in the short term, until enough blacks had gained the skills and expertise to run the country's economy.

The 100,000 or so whites who remained were allowed to keep their land, property, and businesses. Although only 2 percent of Zimbabwe's population of 9 million are white, they still control as much as 80 percent of the country's wealth. They run most of Zimbabwe's industries, and they grow the tobacco that earns the country a good portion of the precious foreign exchange it needs to buy imports. Ian Smith was even permitted to remain in Parliament.

Ndebele "dissidents" surrender to local authorities under amnesty offered by the government in 1988. Tessa Colvin

Whites and blacks try socializing for the first time at Independence Day celebrations, 1980.   Times Media Ltd

White Zimbabweans responded to the new government's overtures in a variety of ways. Many—32,000 between independence and October 1981—left Zimbabwe. Some went to Britain, others to Australia and the United States, but most ended up in South Africa, the continent's last white-ruled state. Despite Mugabe's assurances, many believed that it was only a matter of time before their property was confiscated and their jobs given to blacks. Others could not stomach living under a government led by "terrorists," nor did they care to live in integrated suburbs and send their children to integrated schools. Recently, some of these émigrés have started to return, reassured by Mugabe's moderation.

Those who have stayed have discovered, for the most part, that living under the man they once considered the devil incarnate isn't quite as bad as they anticipated. After years of being deluged with the anticommunist propaganda of the Smith government, they now hardly blink an eye when they hear the leaders of their country addressing each other as "comrade." Most have grown used to having black neighbors, and they can still afford servants, albeit at a slightly higher price. Few, however, have whole-heartedly embraced the new order. Until the thirty white parliamentary seats (ten in the Senate, twenty in the House of Assembly), guaranteed for seven years under the Lancaster House agreement, were abolished in 1987, most white voters stuck with Smith and his party, the Conservative Alliance of Zimbabwe.

On a more personal level, however, cracks are beginning to appear in the wall of white solidarity. There are now white members of ZANU-PF, and people who in 1980 could never envision mixing socially with blacks now have black friends. Those white children being educated in integrated public schools are finding it even easier. Black and white teenagers mix easily at discotheques in the cities, although cross-racial dating and marriage are still rare, because black as well as white parents disapprove.

Unity

One of President Mugabe's greatest triumphs since independence has been his success in ending the ethnic tensions between the Shona and Ndebele that threatened to plunge the country once more into civil war. The Patriotic Front alliance that ended white Rhodesia fell apart almost before the ink was dry on the Lancaster House agreement. The election

Robert Gabriel Mugabe

When the prisoners at the Sikombela detention center heard in 1964 that Robert Mugabe was to be imprisoned there, they built him a thatched hut and painstakingly wove reeds together to make a door. They understood that he was a man who valued his privacy, and they wanted to show how much they respected him. When Mugabe arrived, many were surprised. They had been expecting a powerful, charismatic figure, but instead they found a short, reserved, bespectacled man who looked more like the schoolteacher he had, until recently, been.

Robert Mugabe has changed little since those days. Despite his status as an African Premier, he still values his privacy and he is still an intellectual. By any measure, he is an enigma: an idealist forced by circumstance to be practical, a thinker thrust before the glaring footlights of the world's stage. To Ian Smith he is "an apostle of Satan," to most black Zimbabweans he is a revered liberator.

Perhaps Mugabe's austere and aloof demeanor has something to do with the many difficulties he has had to endure throughout his life. He was born in 1924 in a Trust Land, the son of a poor laborer, and was sent to the local mission school run by Roman Catholic priests. When he was ten, his father went to South Africa to work in the gold mines and never returned. Robert's mother was left alone to bring up her four sons and one daughter.

Robert loved school and was obviously very intelligent. His teacher, Father O'Hea, described him as having "an exceptional mind and an exceptional heart." Today he has six university degrees.

While at Fort Hare University Mugabe was influenced by the South African nationalist leader Nelson Mandela, and also by white Communists who urged him to read the works of Karl Marx. Slowly, he came to see socialism as more Christian than capitalism, which he thought of as enslaving black people. His political education was furthered in 1958 when he went to Ghana, which, under Kwame Nkrumah, had gained its independence the previous year. There he also met Sally Hayfron, who was to become his wife.

Mugabe's own political career began in 1960, when he returned to Southern Rhodesia. He proved a popular speaker, not because he was a great orator but because of what he had to say. The people, he told them, must join together in one nationalist movement, regardless of class, education, or ethnic group. They must be proud of their African heritage, he said, and he encouraged them all to take off their ties and jackets and shoes to symbolize their rejection of the white culture. When Sally gave birth to a boy in 1963, the Mugabes named him Nhamodzenyika, which means "suffering country."

Mugabe was not to know his son. The new father was arrested in 1964, and in 1966 his son died in Ghana of encephalitis. Mugabe pleaded with Smith to allow him to go to his son's funeral, promising to return to prison afterward, but Smith denied his request.

that followed was a lesson not so much in democracy as in demographics. The majority Shona rallied behind Mugabe and ZANU-PF, and the minority Ndebele opted for ZAPU and its leader, Joshua Nkomo.

Within two years ZAPU "dissidents"—ex-ZIPRA (Zimbabwe People's Revolutionary Army) guerrillas—had once more taken to the bush

At Sikombela, Mugabe became the head teacher in the prison school, but he did not just teach the other detainees how to read and write. He also taught them how to make decisions through discussion until the whole group had reached a consensus. No one person's will was to be imposed on the others, he taught.

It was the traditional way of leadership, and as President, Mugabe has tried to abide by it. In many ways there is little difference between those theoretical discussions at Sikombela and cabinet meetings among members of the Zimbabwean government. Each person is allowed his or her say before a group decision is reached. Certainly, Robert Mugabe's voice is often one of the strongest, but he likes to lead from behind. It is better, he thinks, that each person believe the decision is his or her own.

After he was released from detention in November 1974, Mugabe rose to the leadership of ZANU. With his harsh Marxist rhetoric and militant manner, he came to represent everything feared by white Rhodesia. For years they had been told there was a Communist behind every bush, and now he had a face: Robert Mugabe's.

Success has not softened Zimbabwe's President. He is respected rather than loved by his countrymen. A fanatically hard worker, he is still driven by his dream to create a socialist state.

to protest what they saw as unfair treatment of Nkomo and the Ndebele people. What sparked off the rebellion was the dismissal of Nkomo and other ZAPU cabinet ministers after the government charged that ZIPRA had secretly hidden large arms caches to use in a coup against Mugabe. He came down hard on the dissidents and other Ndebele. It is estimated

Joshua Nkomo

In 1987, when Joshua Nkomo finally conceded that he was never to be Zimbabwe's leader, he said, "Now, rather than saving my face, I am saving the face of my country."

He had been asked to make the ultimate political sacrifice and had made it, showing that old Father Zimbabwe, as Nkomo liked to call himself, was what he had always claimed to be: a patriot who put the interests of his country first.

It was the concluding note in his long and illustrious career as one of Zimbabwe's foremost nationalists. For many years he was favored to become the country's first black Premier, and it was through him that many people in the outside world first learned what black people in Rhodesia wanted.

Unlike Mugabe, Nkomo is a leader who inspires love as well as respect from his followers. He has that quality desired by all politicians, "the common touch." He can talk to all types of people in words they understand. As such, he has always posed a threat to the less charismatic Mugabe, and the two have a long history of antagonism.

Nkomo was born in 1917 on a native reserve in Matabeleland. His political career began in 1947 when he became involved in the black railway workers' union. He was soon recognized as a leader in African politics. Believing that he could best serve that nationalist movement by advertising the plight of the country's blacks to the

that between 1982 and 1985 the army, in particular the North Korean-trained Fifth Brigade, killed at least fifteen hundred people, and detained and tortured hundreds of other government opponents. For their

outside world, he spent much of the early 1960's traveling abroad, but was criticized for spending too much time away from Southern Rhodesia. It was criticism of his leadership that lead to the break off of ZANU from ZAPU. It was at this point that the nationalist struggle began to split along ethnic lines, something that proved ultimately politically fatal to Nkomo, a member of the minority Ndebele.

Like Mugabe, Nkomo spent ten years in political detention, and after his release in 1974 he set up his headquarters in Lusaka. The hostility between ZAPU and ZANU, and the fighting between the respective armies, bothered him a great deal. As early as 1970 he had smuggled a message out of jail, begging the two camps to end the "history of disunity among the Zimbabwe people."

"This has created an international atmosphere that is not favorable to our cause, especially since the rival groups are in reality fighting for the same thing," he wrote. "The only difference has been personalities."

Nkomo has always been more compromising than Mugabe. He tried to hold independent negotiations with the Smith government, and although he soon rejected what Smith was offering, the move hurt him politically. He was devastated in 1980 when ZAPU fared so badly in the elections. In 1982 he went into exile in London, and it appeared he might never return to Zimbabwe. But return he did, and old and tired, he came to finally accept Mugabe's leadership of the country.

part, the dissidents killed about 860 black civilians, kidnaped and murdered six foreign tourists, and once again terrorized the white farmers and missionaries in Matabeleland. Seventy farmers, more than were killed in the whole country during the civil war, died at the hands of dissidents.

The government's crackdown on ZAPU was hardly an exercise in democracy, but that little concerned Mugabe. He was determined to crush the seeds of an Ndebele rebellion. In 1987 his strategy of "blood and iron" paid off. First he abolished the white seats in parliament, and in the ensuing elections to fill those seats the ZANU-PF candidates, including eleven whites, swept the board. With an overwhelming parliamentary majority, Mugabe was able to push through a constitutional amendment replacing the post of Prime Minister with that of a strong Executive President. Then he moved to crush ZAPU once and for all by banning the party from holding rallies or meetings, arresting ZAPU officials, and raiding the party offices. By November Nkomo knew he was beaten. He agreed to allow ZAPU to be absorbed into ZANU-PF, essentially consigning his own political hopes to the dustbin of history. The "Unity Agreement," as it was called, was toasted with champagne on December 22, 1987.

In April 1988 the new President offered amnesty to all the rebels, inviting them to turn themselves in. Almost all did, including the notorious Gayigusu, "the beast of the bush," whose gang had axed to death sixteen American Pentacostal missionaries and their families the previous November. Nkomo, who for thirty years strove to become Zimbabwe's first black leader, contented himself with half a loaf. He became one of two Vice-Presidents and was given a seat in an informal, five-person inner cabinet that advised President Mugabe.

Inside the Party

Making Zimbabwe a one-party state did not free President Mugabe from political opposition. With ZAPU eliminated, some of those within

ZANU-PF felt freer to criticize his consolidation of power. One such figure was Edgar Tekere, a Member of Parliament who was once Mugabe's right-hand man. In October 1988 he was expelled from ZANU-PF after charging that establishment of a one-party state would lead to a dictatorship.

Tekere, who in 1989 tried to start a new party, became the hero of people like Zinyoro because he also criticized the government and ZANU-PF for betraying the revolution, which, he said, was benefiting only top government and party officials who were becoming members of Africa's infamous *wabenzi*, a slang term which literally means "the people of the Mercedes-Benz."

Land Resettlement

Such scandals do nothing to soothe the concerns of the vast majority of Zimbabweans for whom the bicycle is standard transportation rather than the Mercedes-Benz. Trying to match the aspirations of the people with the resources of the country has been President Mugabe's biggest headache.

One of the government's hardest tasks has been resettling black peasant farmers on white-owned land. Nine years after independence, 34 percent of Zimbabwe's land was still owned by 4,300 whites. Only about 40,000 black families had been allocated land, less than a quarter of the 162,000 the government had planned to resettle by 1985. More than 800,000 families remained on the communal lands (formerly the Tribal Trust Lands). With each passing year the problem becomes more urgent because of high population growth—an increase of 3.5 percent a year.

Pressure to confiscate white land is still strong, but Mugabe has

A white commercial farmer harvests corn with his workers.   Afrapix, Impact Visuals

resisted this because he fears it will trigger an exodus of white farmers who still play a dominant role in Zimbabwe's agriculturally based economy. Instead, the government has taken acreage abandoned during the war and bought land from white farmers willing to sell. It can force a farmer to sell only if the land is being underused.

National Security

Along with trying to deal with problems within its borders, the Zimbabwean government has also had to deal with attacks from without. In 1986 the guerrilla war that had raged for twelve years in neighboring

Vukuzenzele,
A Solution to Land Hunger

Sir Garfield Todd, a Prime Minister of Southern Rhodesia in the 1950's, has over the years become identified with trying to improve the life of his black compatriots. After independence he gave nearly 3,000 acres (1,200 hectares) of his land to a group of disabled guerrillas, and they have developed it into a farming cooperative called Vukuzenzele, meaning "Wake Up and Help Yourself." With their families, the war veterans have made this drought-stricken patch of bush into a working farm. They grow fruit and vegetables and have started a poultry-and-hog industry.

Sir Garfield thinks that if every farmer who owns more than 2,500 acres (1,000 hectares) of land makes 5 percent of it available to blacks for twenty years, both land hunger and unemployment could be eased. He first tried to implement a land reform program in the early 1970's when he wanted to carve up thousands of acres of his land into farms for forty-four black farmers. The project had to be abandoned, however, when white farmers in the area protested to the Smith government.

A few other white farmers have tried to help with black resettlement. One set aside land for unemployed members of his workers' families. They got a three-year loan from the Zimbabwe Project, a charitable organization, to buy tools. The loan was repaid the first year.

Such successes in racial cooperation encourage people like Sir Garfield. "We've got people and we've got land," he said. "Somewhere along that line is the solution."

The Declaration of Rights

The Zimbabwean constitution guarantees:

1. The fundamental rights and freedom of the individual
2. Protection of right to life
3. Protection of right to personal liberty
4. Protection from slavery and forced labor
5. Protection from inhuman treatment
6. Protection from deprivation of property
7. Protection from arbitrary search or entry*
8. Provisions to secure the protection of the law
9. Protection of freedom of conscience
10. Protection of freedom of expression**
11. Protection of freedom of association and assembly***
12. Protection of freedom of movement
13. Protection from discrimination on grounds of race, tribe, political opinion, color, or creed****

---

* The authorities can and do search people and their homes without a search warrant.

** Speaking out in public against the government usually invites surveillance and can result in arrest and fines. The news media are government controlled and usually reflect the party line. It is also illegal to express racist opinions.

*** No political parties other than ZANU-PF are legal.

**** ZANU-PF membership is considered essential to gain promotion in government bureaucracy. There have also been accusations by Ndebele that they are discriminated against.

Mozambique between South African-backed Mozambican National Resistance (MNR) rebels and the Marxist Mozambique government began to spill over Zimbabwe's eastern border. Hundreds of Zimbabweans, mostly peasants, have been killed by the rebels who object to the fifteen thousand Zimbabwean soldiers stationed in Mozambique to protect the 180-mile (350-kilometer) road, rail, and oil pipeline that runs from Zimbabwe's border to the port city of Beira. Keeping what is known as the Beira Corridor open is considered vital to Zimbabwean security interests and its efforts to become less economically dependent on white-ruled South Africa.

The government considers the MNR attacks as evidence of South Africa's continued efforts to keep its black neighbors, including Zimbabwe, off-balance. The South African army has launched several raids on targets inside Zimbabwe, allegedly to destroy bases of the African National Congress (ANC), the South African black nationalist organization. (For more on the ANC see *The Land and People of South Africa.*)

By the late 1980's the government was convinced that a widespread South African espionage and assassination network existed within Zimbabwe's white community. Several bomb attacks were made on the homes and offices of ANC members. When five whites and one black were charged with carrying out the attacks, South Africa launched a rescue mission to free them. The attempt failed, but the rescuers escaped in a helicopter stolen by a white Zimbabwean air force officer.

As Zimbabwe heads toward the twenty-first century, its future stability is far from certain. With rising unemployment in the cities, and land hunger in the country, the government is aware that an increasing number of Zimbabweans are becoming tired of waiting for their turn to taste the fruits of independence. The question remains: Can the government redress the injustices of the colonial era any faster without upsetting the delicate balance of the economy?

Socialism Tomorrow

Every morning except Sunday, Jonas Ngwenya leaves his comfortable home in the fashionable suburb of Lincoln Green and drives his new Peugeot station wagon to the furniture store he owns in downtown Harare. It is a large store in the city's prime shopping district and it caters to people just like Ngwenya: members of Zimbabwe's growing middle class.

"This is what independence means to me," Ngwenya said as he surveyed the display floor from his glass-fronted office. "Here in Zimbabwe we talk about socialism and call each other comrade, but what the African wants—what he has always wanted—is the opportunity to live a good life and give his children what he was denied."

Ngwenya's views are typical of many Zimbabweans for whom "the fruits of victory" include the right to own land and a home as well as enjoy luxuries like television sets, automobiles, swimming pools, and servants.

Ezekiel Mutasa, an electronics whiz, who as a boy growing up in a rural village dreamed of going to Japan, started Zimbabwe's first black-owned computer company and now visits Japan regularly.

"We still have to transform this society," he said. "My employees see this company growing and it gives them confidence. Maybe in my own way, I'm helping the transformation."

Hilda Makuyana, a farmer near Mutare, sees herself as part of the same sort of new Zimbabwe. One of the lucky families to be resettled on land formerly owned by a white farmer, the Makuyanas now grow enough corn on their individual allotment to feed the family and sell a hefty surplus. "The peasants want title to their own land," she said. "The government would like us to work on cooperative farms, but that's not what we want. We want to work for ourselves."

Welcome to the revolution, Zimbabwean style. It's not quite what ZANU-PF's Marxist leaders had in mind, but a desire not to cause any jarring jolts in the capitalist economy already in place at the time of independence, coupled with the strong entrepreneurial spirit of Zimbabwe's people, has forced the government to proceed cautiously along the path to socialism. Ten years after independence, the economy was still mostly in private hands. The government had to be satisfied with nibbling at the edges of capitalism by investing in privately owned businesses, increasing its involvement in state-owned companies, and by manipulating the economy.

While some of President Mugabe's critics accused him of not doing enough to redistribute the country's wealth, many people thought he was wise not to meddle too much with the economy he inherited. It is one of the healthiest and most stable in Africa, thanks in part to the

Economic Mini Facts

LABOR FORCE: 3,506,000 (1986), of whom 2,457,000 were engaged in agriculture

AGRICULTURE:

Principal crops: Tobacco, corn, sugarcane, wheat, barley, millet, sorghum, potatoes, cassava, soybeans, oranges, bananas, groundnuts, cotton, tea, coffee

Livestock: Cattle, goats, sheep, pigs, horses, chickens, donkeys, mules

Exports: Tobacco, corn, sugar, cotton, animal and vegetable oils

Imports: Processed food, live animals, animal and vegetable oils

MINING: Over forty different minerals

Principal minerals: Gold, asbestos, chromium, coal, cobalt, copper, iron, nickel, silver, tin

Exports: Most minerals mined, in the form of ferro-alloys, ingots, iron and steel bars, copper metal, nickel metal

MANUFACTURING:	Over 6,000 items
Principal products:	Processed meat and dairy goods, grain, milled products (e.g., flour), soft drinks, alcoholic drinks, cigarettes, clothing, shoes, furniture, paper and board, fertilizers and pesticides, soaps and pharmaceuticals, plastics, rubber, electrical machinery
Exports:	Beverages, cigarettes, machinery and transport equipment
Imports:	Beverages, cigarettes, fuel oil, electricity, insecticides, disinfectants, clothing, iron and steel, machinery, spare parts, bus and truck chassis and parts
TOURISM:	345,640 tourists arrived in 1986
PRINCIPAL TRADING PARTNERS:	South Africa, Britain, West Germany, the United States, Japan, Italy, Botswana, Zambia
FINANCE:	
Currency:	100 cents = 1 Zimbabwe dollar (Z$)
Denominations:	Coins—half cent, 1, 2 and a half, 5, 10, 20, 25, 50 cents, and Z$1.00 Notes—1, 2, 5, and 10 dollars.
United States dollar equivalent (March 1989):	U.S.$1 = Z$1.97

fifteen years of economic sanctions the country endured from 1965 to 1980, which made the country more self-sufficient. Because Rhodesia was unable to obtain many imported goods, it was forced to develop a manufacturing sector almost from scratch. In addition, although the Zimbabwean economy depends most heavily on agriculture, it also has rich mineral resources.

The Commercial Farmers

George Wyden is perhaps the most visible symbol of just how slow Zimbabwe's road to socialism has been. He is one of the country's 4,300 white commercial farmers. For seven years he was on the front line of the civil war, half farmer, half soldier, traveling around his 5,500-acre (2,200-hectare) tobacco farm inside an armored capsule mounted on a truck. Today the capsule is rusting next to Wyden's twenty-eight full tobacco barns, and life for him and his family is better than ever.

His story is typical of Zimbabwe's white farmers, who remain a vital part of the country's economy. Although more than 150,000 whites left Zimbabwe after independence, only seven hundred of them were farmers. A glance at the country's balance sheet explains why these people have been handled with kid gloves by the government. Tobacco vies with gold as Zimbabwe's top export. It earns the country more foreign exchange than any other agricultural product. That foreign currency— American dollars, British pounds, German marks—enables the country to import machinery, spare parts, and other crucial equipment to keep its mining and manufacturing sectors running. But tobacco is a crop that must be grown on a large scale, and it requires great expertise and a lot of expensive equipment to produce. That knowledge and wealth rest securely in the hands of Zimbabwe's white farmers. The government acknowledges that it will take time for Zimbabwe's blacks to learn how to farm on a large scale, and until then the white farmer is considered a necessity.

The government, which wants to encourage people to stay in the rural areas rather than migrating to the cities, also values the white farming sector as an employer. It provides more than 250,000 jobs mainly to people from the communal areas. At independence, a farm laborer's monthly wage was about Z$30 (U.S.$15). By the end of the 1980's, with a minimum wage in force, the average worker's pay had tripled.

The Peasant Farmers

Bettinah Gurajena spends her days bumping along rutted dirt roads on her red Honda motorbike as she visits farmers around the small rural town of Bindura. She is an agricultural extension agent and she, together with the six hundred other agents scattered around the country, is the most visible link between the government and Zimbabwe's 800,000 peasant farmers. It is a job Gurajena takes seriously. Seventy percent of all Zimbabweans depend in some way on farming for their livelihood, and it is through people like Gurajena that they have become Africa's most successful farmers. She and the other agents are a mixture of teacher, messenger, and cheerleader. They teach the peasants how to care for their land and animals, carry news of new developments in agricultural research, and are always on hand to provide advice and encouragement.

The results have been startling. In 1985, when drought was causing millions of deaths around the continent, Zimbabwe grew so much corn that it became the first African country to donate food aid to Ethiopia. By the end of the decade grain silos around the country were overflowing and mountains of neatly stacked sacks of corn were growing up around collection depots. In 1988 Zimbabwe produced about 2 million

Peasant Farming and Land Usage

The traditional relationship Zimbabwe's peasants have toward the land has been profoundly disrupted by white colonization and the changes of the postindependence revolution. Yet land remains central to the identity of many of the country's rural people, as is shown by its importance as an issue in the war of liberation and its aftermath.

This significance is illustrated in a Shona tale in which Mwari, the high god, distributed goods to men. To one man he gave people, to another he gave cattle, and to a third only one handful of soil. This last man was able to claim as his own all that grew in or fell on the soil, including all the people and cattle born on the land.

Traditionally, all the land in a certain area belongs to the chief by right of his ancestral link to the founders of the clan. People often say the real "owners" of the land are the spirit guardians of the chiefdom. To this day many peasant farmers carry on the tradition of *chisi*, days sacred to the spirits, on which people should not work the soil in any way.

Before there was any limit on the land, a man was given his fields by his father with the consent of the village headman. Although women did (and often still do) most of the actual cultivation, the land was allocated to their fathers or husbands. Each year the amount of the field under cultivation was increased until the land was exhausted, at which stage the man would be given a new field.

Today most of the land in communal areas has been allocated, so that shifting cultivation can no longer be practiced. Many families

Herding the family's cattle, a traditional task for young boys.   The Hutchison Library

have no more than five acres, which must be used again and again. Fertilization, crop rotation, and contour ridging (plowing in accordance with land contour rather than across contours) must be practiced if the soil is to be kept productive and erosion prevented.

After independence, women were allowed to own land for the first time, but in the rural areas this is still rare. The household head (the man) officially controls the fields, but the wives, who do most of the farming, frequently are very influential in what is grown and how. The men are also often absent because they have to go to the cities or commercial farms to earn cash wages to supplement their families' incomes.

tons of corn but needed only about 600,000 tons to feed its own people.

This amazing abundance is a source of enormous satisfaction to Gurajena, who remembers the days before independence when most peasant farmers, ignorant of modern farming methods and unable to store surpluses for long, grew only enough for their own needs. Before 1980 the largest corn crop marketed by peasants was 67,000 tons. In those days it was mostly white commercial farmers who benefited from advances in moisture conservation, seed varieties, pest control, and fertilizers. The average African farmer was left to work his or her small plot using traditional methods that were suitable only for the shifting cultivation practiced before white colonization forced the blacks to live in restricted areas.

Even in the face of such success, Zimbabwe faces some daunting problems if it is to continue to feed its growing population into the twenty-first century. Only 10 percent of the peasant farmers own their own farms. The rest still live on communal lands where overcrowding, overcultivation, and overgrazing remain persistent problems. The result is enormous soil erosion—about 40,000 pounds per acre each year. Some Zimbabweans believe that granting land ownership to the people would encourage them to look after their land better.

Socialists, however, advocate organizing the peasants onto self-supporting, state-owned cooperative farms. Granting the people land ownership, they say, would only encourage the more ambitious farmers to buy out others. Some peasants have voluntarily formed themselves into cooperatives, but it is yet to become official government policy.

A woman winnows corn grown in the family fields. Each family is usually allotted about three acres.   Carolyn Watson/Foster Parents Plan International

The Conservationists

When Graham Harris smells the pungent odor of death, he always hopes he will find a zebra killed by lions or a buffalo felled by disease or old age. Too often, however, the sight that meets his eyes when he rounds the corner of one of the ancient game trails he walks daily is enough to turn his stomach. Sometimes it is the rotting carcass of a young elephant, its whole face torn away by poachers in their effort to take its ivory tusks. Or it might be a dead black rhinoceros, one of the precious few left in the world, now gone.

Harris is a game ranger near Mana Pools in the middle Zambezi Valley. He is on the front line of an intense war against some of the most determined and highly organized poachers in the world. Small groups of men carrying high-powered rifles cross the Zambezi River in dugout canoes. Quickly they stalk their prey, shoot it, take the tusks or horns, and make a quick getaway. One reason poachers have targeted Zimbabwe is that it is home to half of the world's remaining black rhino population of 6,000. Just one horn will fetch up to US$15,000 in Southeast Asia and Yemen, where they are used ground up as medicine or as ceremonial daggers. The Zimbabwean government is determined to put a stop to it and rangers, the police, and army have orders to shoot to kill when pursuing poachers.

When a ranger comes across an animal killed by poachers, he and his assistants immediately search both the remains and the surrounding bush for clues. Bullets, pieces of newspaper from across the river in Zambia, an elephant's tail hair (often used for making bracelets), all give hints to who the killers might be. Each object is placed in a small plastic bag and sent to Harare for forensic tests.

Several international organizations, including the Rhino Survival Campaign in the United States, raise money to help equip Zimbabwe's

Tsetse-Fly Control

Although the deadly tsetse fly is now mostly controlled in
Zimbabwe, some wildlife experts are against total eradication of the
parasite because they fear much of the natural, tsetse-infested
habitat of wild game would be destroyed if it became possible to
raise cattle there. Government policy, however, is to kill the fly
wherever it is found. In recent years Zimbabwean researchers, led
by Dr. Glyn Vale, have tried to replace aggressive spraying of DDT,
an insecticide banned in the United States because of its
long-lasting toxic residue, with environmentally safer methods. Dr.
Vale discovered that the flies can be lured into traps baited with the
smell of ox breath. The odor, held by absorbents, is made up of
carbon dioxide, acetone, and octenol. He also found that the tsetse
flies are attracted to pieces of black cloth. With this knowledge, Dr.
Vale has invented a tsetse "trap." The flies are initially attracted to
the trap by a bottle of concentrated "odor of ox breath." As they
approach to investigate the odor, they fly toward the black cloth
kites and get caught in nets impregnated with insecticide.

antipoaching units with trucks, radios, patrol boats, and aircraft. But the
government fears it may be fighting a losing battle. It is not permitted
to pursue the poachers across the Zambezi, and Zambia does not have
the same commitment to stamping them out as Zimbabwe, possibly, it
has been alleged, because senior Zambian officials are directly involved
in the horn and tusk trafficking.

Another way Zimbabweans conserve their rich wildlife heritage is by game farming. Farmers in drier areas like Matabeleland and the lowveld have discovered that nurturing the wide variety of antelope that populate the country provides a good source of income to supplement ordinary cattle ranching. Under the watchful eye of the Wildlife Producers' Association, ranchers might cull herds for venison, allow judicious hunting (it costs as much as Z$1,000—US$500—to shoot a single kudu), or run photographic safaris. Some antelope are captured and sold live to overseas zoos. If any species is in danger of becoming extinct, the Association will press for the animals to be placed on a protected list. There are almost 10 million acres (4 million hectares) of national parks, sanctuaries, botanical reserves, and safari areas in the country.

The Businesspeople

Philemon Mushi is the owner of what should be a thriving taxicab business in Bulawayo. With people flooding to the city from the countryside and a shortage of public transportation, he does not lack customers. But three quarters of Mushi's fleet of taxis stand idle, and he fears that soon none will be operational. His problem is a common one in Zimbabwe's business community. He cannot get spare parts to fix his cabs because the country suffers from a severe foreign exchange shortage. This means that the government does not have enough foreign currency with which to buy imported goods. This acts as a severe brake on economic growth in Zimbabwe. Farmers, unable to get parts for their tractors and combine harvesters, have to grow less and employ fewer people. Mines and industries can operate at only partial capacity and

Although many people do want their own land, many others make a successful living on cooperatives. Here, at Guqukani cooperative in Matabeleland, a man mends soccer balls.
Biddy Partridge

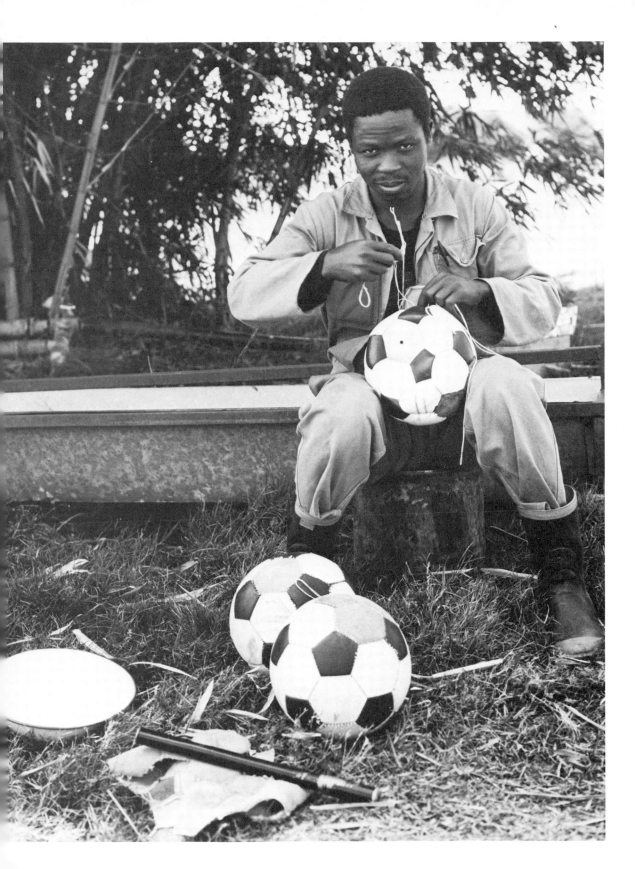

H. J. Heinz Co., an American Company in Zimbabwe

Heinz, the Pittsburgh-based manufacturer of processed foods, was the only American company to invest in Zimbabwe in the first ten years after independence. In 1982 it bought Olivine, a local firm that made candles, soap, vegetable oil, and margarine, for US$25 million. It was a purchase that required considerable persistence on the part of Heinz, mostly because the government insisted on buying a majority stake in the local company. Heinz held out, however, and today it owns a 51-percent share. It also demanded that the government lift the limits it had imposed on the price of cooking oil before signing the deal.

With the government owning 49 percent of Olivine, four government representatives sit on the company's nine-member board of directors. Heinz does not see this as an example of government meddling. Instead, it views it as an advantage because the government directors have been able to help shepherd the company through the bureaucratic tangles that sometimes arise in a country where those in power are keen to exert control over the economy.

So far Heinz considers Olivine a good investment. It spent US$10 million to double the capacity of the plant to produce soap and edible oils and today dominates the candle, soap, and vegetable oil markets. To be sure, it has faced difficulties not encountered in the United States. With twenty thousand whites leaving the country every year, it has had trouble finding skilled labor to replace them. In addition, for two months Olivine lacked seeds for the vegetable oils because of drought.

consequently have to scale back their operations. On a day-to-day basis Zimbabweans battle with a constant shortage of consumer goods, from toothpaste to laundry detergent to car tires. The situation would be even more critical if Zimbabwe did not manufacture so many goods domestically.

Zimbabwe's problems stem from several sources. After independence, the government borrowed heavily from foreign banks to finance the social programs it instituted to help redress the injustices of the past. New schools and clinics popped up around the country and the government vastly increased the size of its bureaucracy to provide more jobs. The army tripled in size and defense spending skyrocketed as Zimbabwean soldiers were dispatched to safeguard the trade route through Mozambique. Resources were further drained by inefficient state organizations that marketed grain, milk, beef, and other products and that ran the railroad, airline, and iron and steel industries. By the end of the 1980's Zimbabwe's loans began to come due, and it had to repay them in precious foreign currency. The result was that the government was forced to allow private industry to buy only a small amount of foreign exchange with which to buy imported goods.

Many of Zimbabwe's businesspeople see the solution to the country's economic problems, including its rising unemployment, in attracting foreign investment. This has proven a sticky issue with the more socialist-minded people in the government. Since 1980 there has been very little new foreign investment, mostly because American and European businesspeople fear that the Zimbabwean government will nationalize private businesses (i.e., transfer ownership to the state). In addition, the government has shown an increasing tendency to become more involved in private industry, and through its investment arm, the Industrial Development Corporation (IDC), it tries to buy a majority stake in foreign-owned companies.

Miners in a gold mine near Chegutu inspect their work.   Zimbabwe Ministry of Information

The Workers

Every weekday morning Jonathan Mbizvo gulps down his breakfast cereal and rushes to the bus stop, where he is picked up before 6:30 A.M. and taken to the industrial section of Harare. He is not expected at his job in a food processing plant until eight o'clock but Mbizvo, who daily passes the lines of unemployed people at the factory gates, likes to get there early. "I'm terrified of getting the sack," he says.

Mbizvo is not alone in his fear of being fired, although, as he will quickly acknowledge, the Zimbabwean government has gone a long way to ensure that he will keep his job. Employers have to give good reason for firing employees and must pay unionized factory workers a monthly wage of at least Z$85 (US$43) a month.

Despite regular pay raises Mbizvo has found his income has not kept up with inflation, and he sometimes feels that life for people like him has not changed much since independence. He lives with his wife and three children in what was once "township" housing: a small one-bedroom house on an unpaved road. The black middle class that now

Worker in textile factory.   Zimbabwe Ministry of Information

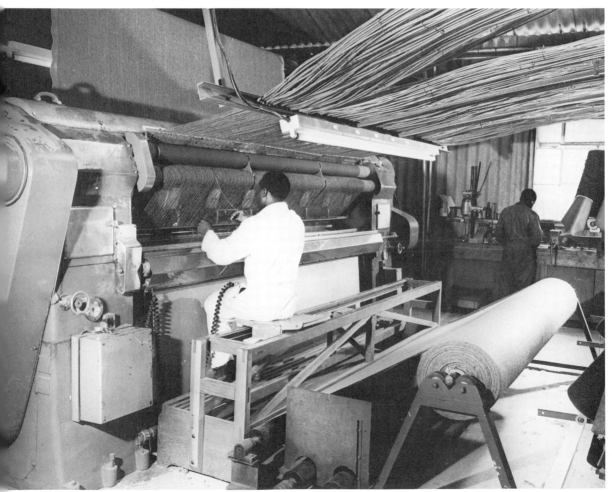

lives in the formerly "white" suburbs seem as distant from him as the whites once were. But Mbizvo is hopeful that the gap is narrowing. In 1986 the government put a wage freeze on everyone earning over Z$36,000 (US$18,000) a year. Wage rises for those paid less take place on a graduated scale, from those earning Z$30,000–Z$36,000 (US$15,000–US$18,000) getting a 3-percent raise a year to those earning Z$1,200–Z$3,500 (US$600–US$1,750) getting an annual raise of 10 percent.

Whether a Zimbabwean earns Z$3,000 or Z$30,000, he or she is uncomfortably aware that the country's economic livelihood depends on South Africa, the white-ruled industrial giant to the south. Not only does South Africa own a large proportion of Zimbabwe's mining industry, but South Africa is also Zimbabwe's largest trading partner, buying about 18 percent of the country's exports and supplying about 20 percent of its imports. In addition, 70 percent of landlocked Zimbabwe's trade moves to South African ports along its road and rail system, and the state-owned Air Zimbabwe needs its South African routes to remain profitable. The country also has no cost-effective way of making steel without South African coking coal. Without it the state-owned steel company, Zimbabwe's largest employer, would have to close down. In short, a trade cutoff between the two countries would be disastrous for Zimbabwe. As one Harare businessman described it: "It's like being in bed with an angry elephant."

The Zimbabwean government periodically threatens to cut off all trade and diplomatic ties with South Africa as a demonstration of its hatred of the white-supremacist regime. The people, President Mugabe once said, would have to tighten their belts and be prepared to eat *sadza* (the staple corn porridge) without *nyama* (meat). So far, however, the Zimbabwean government has not carried out its threat and even maintains a trade agreement with South Africa that makes Zimbabwean goods competitive on the South African market.

Women in Industry

Zimbabwean women are still second-class citizens in the workplace. They are concentrated in the food, clothing, and textile industries, which reflect traditional women's concerns. They do jobs, such as hand-stitching in clothing factories, that are extensions of women's domestic tasks.

Most women get paid less than men for doing the same work. Unable to make ends meet on their small salaries, many women supplement their incomes by selling knitted and crocheted clothing and tablecloths. Others order goods wholesale from the factories in which they work to sell to their friends and relatives. They have fewer promotional opportunities than men and usually find it difficult to move out of unskilled positions.

Few women get paid maternity leave when they have children, which is a severe handicap in a society that favors large families. Zimbabweans traditionally expect the women to perform all the domestic chores. This means that the workday for many begins before 6 A.M. and ends after midnight.

It is very difficult to organize women into trade unions, because they have no time left after doing full-time jobs, running households, and caring for children. Zimbabwean women are also handicapped in that they are, by custom, shy and self-effacing. It is not considered seemly for a woman to thrust herself forward or to complain too strenuously. The few women willing to do so have found themselves struggling alone within male-dominated unions.

In recent years some women have tried to make themselves heard through women's leagues associated with unions. Within this all-female environment women have found it easier to discuss their problems and gain the confidence needed to work toward finding solutions.

Instead, Zimbabwe has joined together with eight other black-ruled countries—Mozambique, Angola, Swaziland, Lesotho, Botswana, Zambia, Malawi, and Tanzania—to form the Southern African Development Coordination Conference (SADCC) in an effort to reduce the region's dependence on South Africa and coordinate regional development policies. SADCC's priority has been to improve three transportation routes that bypass South Africa: the Tazara rail line from Zambia to Tanzania; the Beira Corridor, a rail, road, and oil pipeline running from Zimbabwe to the Mozambican port city of Beira; and the Limpopo railway, running from Zimbabwe to Maputo, the port capital of Mozambique.

If all three can be kept operational, SADCC estimates they could carry 80 percent of the member states' US$10-billion yearly trade and dramatically reduce dependence on South Africa. But it is an expensive commitment costing Zimbabwe about US$1.6 million a week just to keep troops in Mozambique to protect the lines.

The Zimbabwean government's dilemma—that of balancing economic prosperity with fulfilling the promises of the revolution—is not a new one in Africa. What has made it different from many other African countries is that it has succeeded so well.

Serving the People— Promises and Problems

It is barely six A.M. when Elsie Moyo rousts her three oldest children out of bed to get ready for school. Like their counterparts the world over, they grumble and dawdle but they know that even if their mother can be persuaded otherwise in other matters, on the subject of school she is immoveable. Her attitude is not surprising. Elsie can hardly read or write, and she is ashamed of her English. When she was growing up in the late 1950's, she, like 80 percent of Southern Rhodesia's black children, only attended school for three years. Her parents could afford to keep just one of their eight children at school longer than that. By comparison, white children received eleven years of compulsory education.

Today, it is the government's aim to provide free education for every

A white schoolboy teaches his black compatriot to tie his tie after government schools became desegregated. AP/Wide World Photos

Zimbabwean child. With the help of government funding, Elsie and Shadrach Moyo, together with other parents in the neighborhood, built the Kawere School. They did this not with cake sales and raffles, but by literally making the bricks and constructing classrooms and teachers' houses with their own hands. Today, about 950 local children attend the school. As they loiter through the gates, a large sign reminds them that "Knowledge Is Power."

An American child would find the Kawere School very primitive. There are no laboratories or libraries, no gymnasiums or halls. The students, who go from Sub A (grade one) through Form Four (grade eleven), often have no desks and must share books. There are no tennis courts or playing fields either. Instead, the students have a vegetable garden and a peanut field. To learn how to combat soil erosion, they grow trees. Along with the usual problems of bullying and teen pregnancy, Kawere also has a problem with goats and wild pigs occasionally rampaging through the school garden.

To Elsie and the other parents, the school is the most tangible evidence that a revolution has taken place in Zimbabwe. In the first ten years after independence, the number of children in schools more than tripled, from 900,000 in 1980 to over 3 million in 1990. Due largely to the rural building program, the number of schools has gone from 2,177 in 1979 to 5,784 in 1989. The cost to the government has been enormous. In the first five years of independence, the education budget increased 356 percent.

Nevertheless, the country's educational facilities are still hopelessly overburdened. Many schools, built to hold eight hundred students, now have twice that number enrolled. The problem is particularly bad in the urban areas where formerly whites-only schools now cater to everyone. Some schools have had to introduce a system of "hot seating" in which one group of students attends classes in the morning and then leaves to make room for others in the afternoon.

There is also a shortage of qualified teachers. About half of all primary-school teachers are untrained, and many have not even graduated from high school. To remedy the problem, the government has recruited teachers from overseas, mostly Britain, Australia, and West Germany. It has also set up an on-the-job training program.

At independence, the new government hoped to carry the revolution in education beyond just school building. It also planned to change what was taught in the schools. A unit was set up in the Education Ministry to revise the school curriculum and textbooks to reflect the govern-

Villagers work together to build a school. Once the walls are erected, the government pays for the roof. Carolyn Watson/Foster Parents Plan International

ment's socialist ideology, and an organization called the Zimbabwe Foundation for Education and Production (Zimfep) pioneered the "education with production" principle. This advocated teaching practical subjects—like farming, construction, and carpentry—along with the usual academic subjects. Zimfep set up eight farm schools that housed and educated thousands of war orphans and refugees returning from neighboring countries.

The government would like to institute the Zimfep program in all public schools, but so far it has not been possible. The main reason for this is that most Zimbabweans want exactly the same education as the whites were given and blacks were denied before 1980. They see manual labor as a symbol of their old life under white bosses and have acquired the white prejudice that a technical education is for the less intelligent.

Because this attitude is so prevalent, Zimbabwe's education curriculum is still built around the British system of "O" and "A" Level examinations that were the backbone of the preindependence education system. Students usually take their "O"—Ordinary—Levels when they are sixteen or seventeen. This involves testing them on two years' worth of work in seven or eight subjects. To pass "O" Levels, the student must pass at least five subjects, including English language and mathematics. If a student wants to go to a university, he or she must study an additional two years for "A"—Advanced—Levels, which means studying only two to four subjects in depth, usually in the same discipline (arts or sciences). All of these examinations are composed and marked in Britain. Not surprisingly, the subject matter is heavily oriented toward Europe.

The government would like to change the system, because not only is much of this curriculum irrelevant to Zimbabweans, but it also puts Africans at a disadvantage because their home language is usually not

Mapfure College— One Zimfep Project

Mapfure College, located 60 miles (108 kilometers) from Harare near Chegutu, caters specifically to ex-guerrillas who emerged from the war without an education or job skills.

The school combines basic academic subjects with vocational and technical training. English, math, and socialist-oriented political economy are taught along with agriculture, technical services, and running collective farms and businesses. The emphasis is on practical application. Students in the building class, for example, learn simple architectural drafting and building design, and construct model homes and other buildings on the college campus.

In most ways Mapfure is a success, but it suffers from many of the problems encountered by other Zimbabwean schools: not enough money, equipment, or qualified teachers. Like other Zimfep projects, Mapfure receives more money per student from the government than regular public schools, but even this has not been enough to avert the problem of too many students and not enough tools. One lesson Zimfep has learned at Mapfure is that a good vocational education requires expensive equipment. For this reason, the Zimbabwean government is pessimistic about its financial ability to put into place nationwide the Zimfep model of education.

English and their cultural background is very different from that of English children. "The standard world history taught is still that European history is the center of everything," one teacher complained. "In biology, when we talk about plants or animals, the examples in the textbooks are always something familiar in Britain and not here.''

The failure rate among black Zimbabweans taking these examinations is high—fewer than 40 percent pass their "O" Levels—and the country's leaders continue to press for an abandonment of the system in favor of something that will raise African socialists rather than European capitalists. Those in favor of a change also argue that the emphasis on academic rather than practical subjects is contributing to the growing unemployment problem by leading most school graduates to expect white-collar desk jobs.

For most whites, the revolution in Zimbabwe's education system has meant only one thing: expensive school fees. As black children have flooded once-whites-only government schools, Zimbabwe's whites have withdrawn their children and sent them to expensive private schools. There they can still enjoy the advantages of a privileged education, away from the overcrowding and shortages of the public school system. This has infuriated the government, which tried to insist that private schools have a majority of black students. So far, however, these elite schools remain mostly white. Many have two-year waiting lists, and some whites even put their children's names on these lists as soon as they are born.

Health

Elsie Moyo clearly remembers when her daughter Ruth came down with a bad stomach complaint. The first thing she did was strap the child securely to her back with a towel and carry her eight miles to the mission hospital. There, the white doctor gave the child some medicine and told Elsie to make sure that from now on she gave Ruth only clean water that had been boiled. He also told her to give the child more

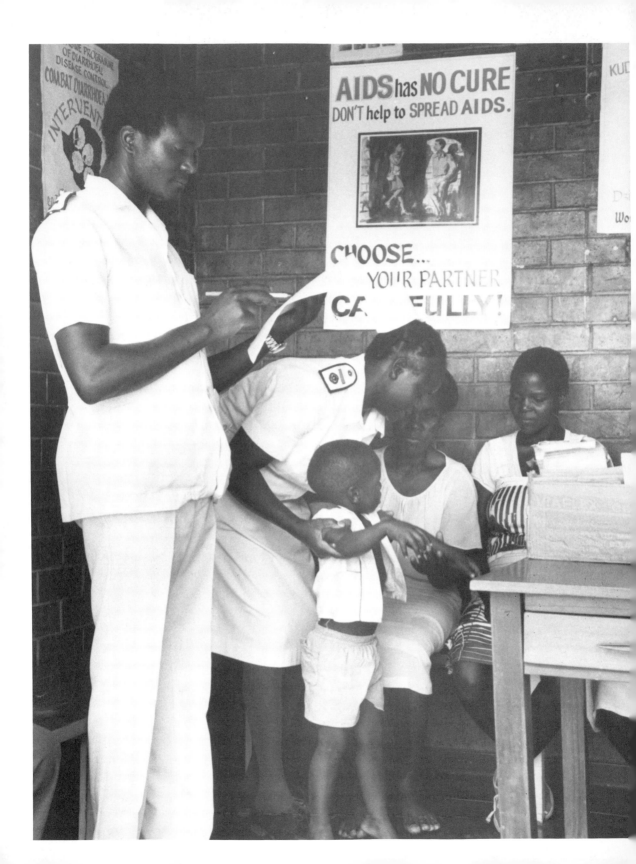

vegetables and less *sadza* because her stomach could not digest the stiff corn porridge.

The next day Ruth was much better, but as far as Elsie was concerned, nothing had yet been done to *really* get to the root of the problem. As soon as she had finished her morning chores, she once more set off, but this time instead of turning toward the main road, she hurried down a dusty path toward a neighboring village. She was going to visit the *n'anga* (traditional diviner-healer), who would be able to tell her why the ancestral spirits had given little Ruth this illness and how she could appease them. Elsie had great faith in this *n'anga*, who had given her excellent advice in the past about all kinds of problems and had even supplied her with a love potion that had helped her ensnare Shadrach.

Upon reaching the neighboring village, Elsie greeted the *n'anga* with respect and squatted down opposite him in silence. It was not necessary for her to tell him why she had come, because she assumed the spirit that possessed the *n'anga* would have already told him. After collecting his fee, the *n'anga* began to talk to Elsie, carefully watching her reactions to his statements and questions. Then he drew out his divining dice, four carved pieces of wood, and began to throw them on the dusty patch of ground at his feet. Each die had a separate meaning and, by carefully watching what side up they landed and in what combinations, he eventually "divined" why Elsie's ancestral spirits were angry with her.

"You say you have been very busy harvesting your corn, Elsie?" the *n'anga* asked. "Can it be you have forgotten to honor the spirit elders?"

Elsie felt a twinge of guilt. It had indeed been a long time since she

Posters in clinics around the country warn the people about the danger of AIDS. Carolyn Watson/Foster Parents Plan International

Becoming a N'anga

To become a *n'anga*, a person must give evidence that he or she has the help of a healing spirit. Often this is the spirit of a dead close relative who was a *n'anga* during life and wishes to continue his or her work through a living descendant.

Usually, the first indication a person has that he or she is destined to be a *n'anga* is a dream in which the host sees himself or herself practicing as a diviner or healer. This is usually also accompanied by an illness, often a mental illness, during which the spirit asks to enter the sick person. Often, there is a traditional healing spirit inherited down the generations of one family, and a future *n'anga* may, as a child, receive informal training from his or her predecessor. Many, however, receive no training and learn their art entirely through dreams. In legends, some *n'anga* apparently were instructed by ancestral spirits while living with them at the bottom of pools or riverbeds.

Once the people have accepted the prospective *n'anga*'s experience as genuine, they hold an initiation ceremony in which beer is brewed in honor of the healing spirit. The new *n'anga* usually becomes possessed by the spirit during the singing and dancing that lasts through the night. In the morning, the *n'anga* is consecrated by having his or her hair ritually cut. To acquire a regular clientele, however, the *n'anga*, like an ordinary doctor, has to build up a good reputation.

A possessed spirit medium. The axes held by the two men at the back are tsomho, or *"dancing axes," and are very popular at religious ceremonies.* Zimbabwe Ministry of Information

had brewed the ritual millet beer for Grandfather Moyo. The *n'anga*, who had been watching her face, nodded confidently. "Yes, Elsie, you must hurry back to your *kraal* and do your duty."

It was with a light heart that the woman returned to her own homestead. She gave Ruth the herbal remedy given her by the *n'anga* and prepared a little grain in a gourd cup. That evening when Shadrach returned home, he took the cup and formally addressed his long-dead grandfather. "Grandfather Moyo, here is your grain. We are brewing the beer you have asked for. Make your grandchild well and stop causing trouble in the home."

Elsie attributed Ruth's lasting recovery to this ritual, not to the medicine she was given at the hospital. The Shona rely heavily on modern western medicine, but many see it as merely relieving the symptoms of an illness rather than curing it. Many *n'anga* have some knowledge of herbalism, but since the ultimate cause of disease is seen as spiritual, most of their medical remedies have no basis in science.

From a western point of view, traditional medicine is seen as most useful when treating psychosomatic disorders, helping mental problems, and calming those with terminal illnesses. The clients of the traditional healers totally believe the healers have the help of a healing spirit. Even more sophisticated people, who have long lived in the cities and depended on western medicine, will go to a *n'anga* in times of crisis. In Harare and Bulawayo traditional healers (many of whom have exchanged the paraphernalia and dramatic ritual found among rural *n'anga* for the white coat and consulting office of the medical doctor) make healthy livings from clients who nowadays might publicly claim not to believe in them.

Today, many *n'anga* belong to the Zimbabwe National Traditional Healer's Association. Through this organization, they try to regulate the practice and weed out healers who do more harm than good.

Witchcraft

A belief in witchcraft permeates every level of Shona society. When something bad happens—a person drowns, a man loses his job, a baby dies—witchcraft is often suspected. Witches are usually women who are believed to be possessed by evil spirits. They have many of the same characteristics as witches do in other societies, like wandering around at night performing horrible deeds, keeping familiar beasts of the night such as hyenas, owls, antbears, and snakes, making evil potions, and flying great distances at night. Some Shona also believe a witch will enter a person's hut at night, remove the sleeping victim's head, play soccer with it, and replace it at the end of the game, all without the person knowing about it. They are also supposed to be very fond of eating human flesh, especially the flesh of children. For this reason infertile women, and women whose children die young or who frequently miscarry, are sometimes suspected of deliberately killing their children for the purposes of witchcraft.

While some women admit to being witches, the Shona believe an evil spirit can speak and act through an unwilling human host. Sometimes these hosts don't even know they are witches until a diviner identifies them as such. Some prospective hosts may try to refuse to accept the evil spirit by having a traditional healer transfer it into a chicken or goat, which is driven away into the wild. Once a witch has accepted the spirit, she is considered virtually incurable because she comes to enjoy doing evil.

One of the Zimbabwean government's top priorities since independence has been to build more rural clinics and hospitals in an effort to combat malnutrition and a high rate of infant mortality among peasants. It has proven an uphill battle. Medical facilities before 1980 were heavily concentrated in the cities. Most peasants did not have clean drinking water, proper toilets, or an adequate diet. In some areas 220 black children out of every 1,000 died before reaching the age of five. By comparison, only 17 white children out of every 1,000 died. The diseases suffered by the two races also reflected their different life-styles. Whites were most often victims of heart disease and cancer, illnesses usually associated with a high standard of living. Blacks died of dysentery, typhoid, diarrhea, and other waterborne diseases, reflecting the poor sanitation of the rural areas.

At independence, the new government set about trying to build a rural health center no farther than 5 miles (8 kilometers) from each person. In the same way that communities were encouraged to build their own schools, the people were also encouraged to build their own clinics. The government set about training village health workers in basic preventive medicine and tried to place responsibility for the construction of toilets, clean wells, and healthy living quarters on the rural community. All these efforts have borne some fruit—infant mortality is now about 60 deaths per 1,000—but the problems of poverty continue to plague many Zimbabweans.

In the rural areas within sight of overflowing grain silos children die daily from kwashiorkor and other diseases of malnutrition. A 1986 United Nations Children's Fund report estimated that 30 to 48 percent of Zimbabwe's under-five population suffered from malnutrition. The reason can be found in a mixture of poverty and politics. In its drive to earn foreign exchange, the government has encouraged peasants to grow export crops at the expense of traditional crops—peanuts, millet,

Three friends share a joke outside a country store, a common place for people to socialize.
Biddy Partridge

and sorghum—that were once relied on for a balanced diet. Despite one of the most up-to-date family-planning programs in Africa, Zimbabwe still has one of the highest birth rates in the world. Overcrowding in the poorly ventilated huts in which many peasants sleep encourages the spread of infection. In recent years, a new scourge has begun to afflict Zimbabweans: AIDS (acquired immune deficiency syndrome). While it has not yet reached epidemic proportions, health officials fear spread of the disease is being accelerated by the continued influx of migrant labor from Zambia and Malawi, both nearby AIDS hotspots.

Life for Workers on White Farms

Among those blacks living in the worst conditions are peasants who work on the large white commercial farms. A study done in Mashonaland West, the district with the highest proportion of commercial farm workers, highlighted their plight. The average monthly income for a family of six was about US$50, most of which was spent on food. Over 20 percent of the workers had no access to functioning toilets, and the average number of people using each toilet was forty. Nearly half the children under age five suffered from diarrhea, which often contributes to malnutrition and dehydration.

On one typical farm the white owners lived within an eight-foot-tall chain-link fence in a large farmhouse with running water, electricity, a septic tank, and all the modern household appliances. Outside the fence, about forty-two black families—about 250 people in all—lived in crowded one-room huts. They had access to four toilets and all had to draw their water from one pump, which had a blocked drain. To get to the pump, the children had to walk through a stagnant swamp infested with mosquitoes, snails, hookworms, and other parasites. Along with diarrhea and dysentery, about fifteen cases of typhoid occur each year.

Not all white farmers neglect their workers to this degree. One farmer spends about $12,000 a year improving conditions for his workers. The eighty families who live on his land have ventilated cottages and electricity. The farmer also gives each family a small vegetable plot and seeds.

Women and children gather water from a borehole for their crops. Drilling boreholes—or open wells—is one way to increase the availability of water to villagers. Carolyn Watson/ Foster Parents Plan International

Justice Mini Facts

VILLAGE
COURT:

1,500 established in 1981 in communal areas to replace old Chief's Courts. Presided over by village elders chosen by the Ministry of Justice. Empowered to deal with cases of minor assault, theft of property of up to Z$50 (US$25) in value, and contraventions of minor bylaws. Can also rule on civil claims of up to Z$200 (US$100), if the claim can be determined under customary law. Can also grant divorces. In 1988 government restored some of the power taken from traditional chiefs at independence.

COMMUNITY
COURT:

300 established in 1981 to replace old District Commissioner's Courts. Can try limited criminal cases and act as courts of appeal for Village Courts. Jurisdiction includes communal areas and commercial farming areas, but it is highly unusual for a white person to be brought before this court.

MAGISTRATE'S
COURT:

Set up in ascending tiers of district, provincial, and regional courts to hear most criminal and civil cases. Acts as court of appeal for Community Courts.

HIGH COURT:

Tries capital offenses.

SUPREME
COURT:

Final court of appeal.

Other specialized courts include: the Juvenile Court, the Maintenance Court, the Income Tax Court, the Town Planning Court, and the Water Court.

Justice

The traditional Shona view of the role of the courts is very different from that of modern westerners. Because the Shona emphasize harmony of the community over individual rights, the overriding concern of their customary law is to reconcile disputing parties rather than to make a judgment in favor of one person over another. In modern Zimbabwe, Shona customary law still plays an important role in the country's system of justice. Many minor cases are resolved in traditional village and community courts. Serious crimes and civil cases are tried under the more rigid western legal system in Magistrate's Courts, Regional Courts, and the High Court. The Supreme Court of Zimbabwe, like the U.S. Supreme Court, is purely a court of appeal.

Family disputes are usually solved within the family, at an informal gathering of the senior men. If the problem cannot be solved at this level, it will then be taken to either a village or a community court.

At these courts both parties in the dispute are expected to present tokens (nowadays usually in the form of court fees) as evidence of their serious intentions and their willingness to abide by the judgment of the court. This is more binding than an oath to the Shona, who believe that one of the purposes of conversation is to be pleasing to the listener. Therefore, a witness would tell a questioner what he or she wanted to hear rather than the truth. Since the aim of the proceeding is to resolve the quarrel without unpleasantness, people also take great care not to say anything that will offend, even if it means not mentioning something crucial to the case.

After both sides have made a formal statement of their cases, the matter is then thrown open for discussion by everyone else present (often the whole village). Usually, over several hours every aspect and argument of the case is thoroughly talked over and a consensus reached

Women and the Law

Until 1982, when the Legal Age of Majority Act (LAMA) was passed, black Zimbabwean women were considered minors throughout their lives unless they were divorced or widowed. Upon marriage, a woman would leave the guardianship of her father and come completely under the guardianship of her husband. This meant that she could not own land, open a bank account, rent a house, or enter into any other contract without the permission of her father, husband, or other male relative. If she was accused of a crime, she had to be represented in court by her guardian, but if convicted, it was she who was punished.

With the passage of LAMA, Zimbabwean women were legally emancipated. Anyone who has reached the age of eighteen is now considered an adult and can vote and enter into any contracts he or she chooses to. Passage of the law was very controversial, because it was seen as going against traditional African values. People argued that parents would no longer be respected and the outcome would

as to who is in the wrong and what should be done about it. The guilty party is then told to compensate the person he or she has injured. Frequently, the case is not closed until both sides are seen to drink beer or take snuff together in a public display of friendship.

The most important aspect of Shona customary law is that it is flexible. Customs are frequently bent to suit a particular occasion and effect a reconciliation. For this reason, crimes like theft are treated as a dispute between two individuals, rather than as a crime against society

be unwanted pregnancies, the seduction of young women, and prostitution. LAMA also clashed with traditional marriage practices (in which men pay a bride-price for their wives) and traditional inheritance laws, which allow only men to inherit property.

Those who support LAMA argue that the realities of modern life make it imperative for women to be able to make their own decisions and act independently. Because so many men work away from home, their wives are left in charge of the fields and are thus, effectively, independent. Many women also leave their traditional homes and move with their husbands to the towns, where they live independent lives. When their husbands die, it is unfair, LAMA supporters argue, for unknown male relatives to inherit the husband's property. Women also wanted to have greater rights over their children, who, under traditional law, can be taken by the husband if there is a divorce.

So far, only a minority of women have enjoyed the advantages of LAMA, mostly because of a lack of education among rural women and the persistence of traditional values in these areas.

as a whole. The dispute is usually solved by forcing the thief to return the property of the victim and also pay compensation to the court. More serious are crimes against spirit guardians of the chiefdom (spirits of past chiefs). This usually happens when someone works the fields on a holy day of rest, desecrates a shrine, or engages in witchcraft or incest. These actions are believed to endanger the whole community.

In modern Zimbabwe, customary law, which works well in small communities, is not adequate to deal with all matters of justice in the larger society where new values, different codes of behavior, and weakening ties among many urban Shona to their traditional roots have lessened the power of the community over the individual. There is a need, therefore, for the more formalized courts familiar to most westerners. In Zimbabwe the code followed is a mixture of English common law and Roman Dutch law, which originated in Holland and came to Zimbabwe via South Africa. Under this code, cases are decided by panels of judges rather than by juries.

Because of the severe shortage of public defenders, people usually have to retain their own lawyers. This means that most Zimbabweans, who cannot afford the cost, have to defend themselves. Only those accused of capital offenses, such as murder, are permitted public defenders.

During the colonial era, many of the traditional Shona institutions were seen as inferior to their European equivalents. The Zimbabwean government has sought to remove that prejudice by encouraging the good aspects of the old ways and making them compatible with modern Western systems of medicine, education, and justice. It was important to do this because the vast majority of Zimbabwe's people are still, to varying degrees, traditional in their outlook. For the government to serve them effectively, it had to take this into account.

CHAPTER X

Voices
of the Ancestors

The first thing Tafara usually sees when she opens her eyes in the morning and looks through the doorway of her hut are the pink-rimmed hills of northeastern Mashonaland. As she lies on her mat in the dark interior, she imagines that the doorway is a frame for a picture through which she steps each day. She never quite knows what will happen in that picture, but there are certain things about it that never change, that haven't changed since Chaminuka and Nehanda stood before the flowing waters of the Zambezi. The spirits of her ancestors are as real to Tafara as her own mother and father. It was Chaminuka and Nehanda who led the Shona people to victory over the white man. It was the spirit of her great-grandfather, Murongazvombo, who helped the family grow a bumper crop last summer. It is the spirit of her grandmother, Togarepi, who will ensure her fertility.

Religion

The belief in the constant presence of the ancestral spirits stands at the very core of Shona life. For the Shona, these beliefs bind the past and the present together, and draw the extended family group into a complex pattern of mutual responsibilities.

There are two types of spirit guardians: the spirit elders of the family (*midzimu*), and the lion spirits who care for the chiefdom as a whole (*mhondoro*). Each home has a shrine to the *midzimu*, the most important of whom is the father or grandfather of the oldest living generation. Tafara's family honors Grandfather Murongazvombo every year with a ceremonial offering of home-brewed millet beer. Occasionally, when something goes wrong—for example, if someone becomes very ill or loses his or her job—the family approaches Grandfather Murongazvombo, through his medium, an uncle of Tafara's, to ask him why he is displeased. It may be because members of the family are quarreling or the spirit feels he is being forgotten. Usually, an offering of millet beer and promises to do better are enough to appease him. While the spirits of dead female members of the family also have roles to play in the affairs of the living, they seldom are official spirit guardians.

The *mhondoro* or lion spirits, the spirits of clan founders, are more important than the *midzimu*, and they generally concern themselves with matters that affect communities rather than individuals. They are consulted when their domain is plagued by locusts, when lions are preying on the community, when the people are threatened by an epidemic, or when they are about to become involved in a war. Through a possessed medium, an *mhondoro* may announce it has caused the problem because the people are forgetting their ancestors, or perhaps it will accuse members of the community of a specific crime like incest or quarreling at the spirit's shrine.

The Shona, like Christians, believe in an all-powerful God. He is usually known by the name Mwari. Unlike the Christian God, however, Mwari is not interested in the petty lives of individuals, although he is ultimately responsible for everything that happens. The Shona rarely speak of him or try to communicate with him, except in the Matopo

Members of an African independent church, dressed typically in the sect's "uniform."
The Hutchison Library

The Influence of Christianity

Christianity has touched the lives of most Zimbabweans, although only about 25 percent profess to be Christians. Instead, many Shona have accepted certain aspects of Christianity, particularly with regard to their relationships with strangers and new experiences. In this way, many people casually mix traditional religion with Christianity. As one Shona man said: "It's best to believe in it all."

While there are Shona and Ndebele who are devout Christians, many accepted baptism as a means of gaining access to education and Western health care, which, in many missions, was offered only to Christians. Other people sometimes see affiliation with a Christian church as a way of showing themselves to be more advanced than their neighbors. In the cities people use church services as a way of building up social relationships lost when they left their rural villages. Often these people will turn to traditional religion when serious illness or some other disaster strikes.

Church views on certain issues have proved stumbling blocks for many would-be Christians. Chief among these is marriage. Many Shona are not prepared to be married, especially if there is no possibility of divorce later, without first finding out if the proposed

Hills, where there is an organized cult of Mwari. The most influential shrine is at Matónjeni. It is looked after by a high priest and priestess and receives tribute from the Ndebele and even from neighboring white farmers who are interested in covering all their bases to ensure regular

wife can conceive. This means engaging in sex before marriage, something definitely frowned upon by most churches. The result is that many have a church wedding only after the birth of the first child, making a Christian service merely an extra rite in the long process of a traditional marriage.

The influence of the church diminished during the civil war because nationalist guerrillas, often embracing antireligious, anti-Western, Marxist ideology, waged an intense propaganda war against mission churches.

New Independent African Churches

Some Shona, seeking to find something between traditional religion and Christianity, have turned to African independent churches, similar to those founded in the United States by American blacks. There are over one hundred independent churches in Zimbabwe with a following of about half a million people.

Many of these sects emphasize inspiration and revelation by the Holy Spirit often through "speaking in tongues," something that is very familiar to the Shona with their tradition of spirit possession. Followers of these churches often interpret the Bible in the light of traditional values and beliefs.

rainfall. The shrine is a cave from which the voice of Mwari speaks its oracles. The "voice" is an elderly woman who speaks to visiting delegations in a supposedly ancient dialect that must be translated into the language of the visitors.

Family Relationships

After she has slipped on her dress and tied her scarf around her head, Tafara rouses her brother, Tichagwa, and her sisters, Simbarashe and Tatenda. She hurries them along because the sun is already breaking over the horizon. Outside, Tafara can hear the sounds of the other villagers greeting each other with the almost courtly politeness of Shona people everywhere:

"*Mangwanani.*" (Good morning.)

"*Mangwanani.*"

"*Marara here?*" (Have you slept well?)

"*Ndarara kana mararawo.*" (I have slept if you did also.)

"*Ndarara.*" (I slept.)

After helping Tatenda dress, Tafara walks to the main hut to help her mother. Breakfast is a simple affair. Sometimes it is just bread, other times Martha warms up the leftover *sadza* from the night before. Always there is tea with plenty of milk and sugar.

Not everyone eats breakfast, as it is not a traditional Shona meal. Some keep to the old ways and do not eat until about eleven A.M. When the *sadza* is ready, Tafara takes a plate and a tin mug of hot, sweet tea to Grandfather Chirobo. On many mornings he will eat his breakfast in the main hut with the rest of the family, even though it is traditionally considered unseemly for men to eat with women. But Chirobo knows that in these modern times some of the old rules are not so strictly kept, and for breakfast he is willing to be more flexible. Because he is the *baba mukuru* (great father or headman) of the village, his example is followed by the other men. Although he is not everyone's father, Chirobo is related in some way to most of the people who live there. It is his father, Murongazvombo, who is the spirit guardian of the village.

Shona Manners

—A gift is received by first clapping your hands together in a gesture of thanks, and then taking the gift with both hands to show that it is too large for one hand only.

—A gift is given with the right hand, the left hand being unclean.

—You should never stand looking down on another person. It is polite to squat or sit when talking to other people, or to your elders.

—When a man and his family are out together, the man always walks in front, with his hands empty, so that he can protect his brood if need be. His wife walks behind him, carrying everything and keeping the children in hand.

—When approaching a village, you must pause at the edge and shout, *"Svikeyi?"* which means "May we arrive?" When the reply comes back telling you to come on in, then you may proceed.

—When you want to go into someone else's hut, you must stand outside and either clap or shout, *"Gogogoyi,"* which means "Knock, knock, knock."

—Never look another person directly in the eyes.

Despite the changing nature of Shona society, it still remains patrilineal, which means that kinship through males is stressed over kinship through females. A child inherits his or her father's clan name (*mutupo*)

and people distinguish members of their family only by their generation, age, and sex. For example, the term *baba* (father) can apply equally
to a father's brother, male cousin, or any other male of that generation
no matter how distantly they are related.

The individual is not considered important in Shona society. His or
her status and behavior are determined by the relationships that person
has with the other members of the community. The most important
relationship within the Shona family is between father and child. This
is a very formal relationship in which the child always shows the utmost
deference and respect for his or her father. Children can never eat with
their father, take liberties with his property, or address him in a familiar
manner. In contrast, the relationship between mother and child is
extremely close. Most Shona children spend the first few years of their
lives tied securely onto their mothers' backs with towels, and at her
death, a mother's spirit is considered friendly and protective. Because
of her good care for them, not to mention the pains of labor she went
through, a mother's spirit demands to be well remembered by her
children. If they fail to do this, the spirit is believed to regain the same
absolute power over her children that she had when they were in their
infancy.

Marriage

After breakfast Tafara goes to weed the vegetable plot. At eighteen she
no longer goes to school. She is needed at home, because her father lives
and works in Harare. Normally Tafara finds this tedious work, but in
recent months it has become her favorite chore. Her family's fields
border that of a cooperative farm run by a group of former *vakomana*
(guerrillas), and one of these men has recently become her husband-to-

Bathtime in the city. Not all homes have indoor plumbing. Tessa Colvin

· 193 ·

Shona Names

The name of a Shona person provides a wealth of information about its owner. It often reflects how the parents felt at the time of the child's birth, perhaps what the mother's relationship was with her in-laws or the state of the family's fortunes. Possibly a person has a nickname, descriptive of his or her talents or flaws. To illustrate this, here are the meanings of the names of the people introduced in this chapter:

Tafara: We are happy. It describes how her parents felt when she was born.

Tichagwa: We shall fight. Because Tichagwa was born during the war, his parents decided they wanted to show their resolve.

Simbarashe: The power of God. This girl almost died when she was born. Her parents gave her this name to show that Providence was on their side.

Tatenda: We are grateful. This name was given by Tatenda's grandparents, who wanted to thank Martha for yet another child.

be. His name is Chipo, but Tafara likes to think of him by the name he took during the war of liberation: Jekanyika, which means "the one who spends the whole day on the move."

Tafara had first met Chipo in the spring when she was doing the planting. He gave her some seed to grow sorghum after she had mentioned that Grandfather Chirobo liked to chew it. Soon they were meeting regularly. Martha was well aware of these developments, and, after discreetly checking that Chipo was not a rascal, she decided to let nature take its course.

Chirobo: The great talker. Chirobo, who loves company, earned this nickname over his many years as the chief storyteller in the village.

Dakarai: You will be happy. Dakarai's mother had trouble conceiving and gave her child this name to indicate to her husband that she was a good wife who would provide many children.

Murongazvombo: The man who arranges weapons. Chirobo's father earned this name because he was always known to be alert.

Martha and Elias: These two were born in missions and, like many Shona of their generation, they were given biblical names. They gave their children traditional Shona names as a rejection of white values.

Chipo: Gift. He was the only child his mother could have. By adopting the name Jekanyika during the war, Chipo would have been able to hide his true identity from the government and thus protect his family from reprisals by the white government if he had ever been caught. Other guerrillas took names like Teurai Ropa, "spill blood," Ridzai Gidi, "open fire," and Enjoy Chimurenga, "enjoy the struggle."

At first Tafara was afraid that Chipo saw her as just a little girl. One day, however, he put his hand in his pocket and gave her a button from his coat. This was a traditional token of love. It did not indicate that he necessarily wanted to marry her, but it did show that Chipo saw Tafara as a desirable woman. That evening, with great excitement, she showed her friends the button and they discussed at length what Tafara should give Chipo in return. It is customary for the woman to give the man a piece of intimate clothing, and Tafara decided to give him her only nylon petticoat.

The Bride-Price

The bride-price involves two payments. The first, the *rutsambo*, used to be a utility object like a hoe, but now it is usually a large cash payment. This is associated with sexual rights to the woman. After paying the *rutsambo*, the groom usually is permitted to have sexual relations with his wife-to-be. The second payment, the *roora*, involves a second large cash payment or, sometimes, the more traditional payment of cattle.

Although many people believe nowadays that payment of the bride-price is demeaning to women and a form of slavery, it was never perceived as such by the Shona themselves. The husband's family has rights and obligations toward the woman's family, and it may not pass her on to a third party.

The groom may take many years to finish paying the *roora*, partly because it might take him that long to raise it, and partly because he is often disinclined to hand over all the cash until he is fully satisfied that his wife will fulfill all her obligations.

After the exchange of tokens, the romance between Chipo and Tafara was official. Their only point of contention was over how they would proceed to marriage. As citizens of the new Zimbabwe, Chipo believed they should have a modern marriage without all the long-drawn-out negotiations and bride payments of traditional Shona matrimony. Apart from the fact that he saw himself as a man of the future, Chipo disliked the idea of being in debt for years to his father-in-law. Frequently, he quoted the old Shona proverb: "A son-in-law is like a fruit tree: One never finishes eating from it." Tafara, however, was not happy with this. She had always grown up in a traditional setting and she knew that her family would be very unhappy if she just "ran off" with this man (because in their eyes that is what a modern, Western-style marriage amounted to).

With much groaning, Chipo entered into negotiations with Tafara's father, Elias. Elias asked rather a lot for Tafara: Z\$500 and a new set of clothes for himself and Martha. But as he pointed out, Tafara was his oldest daughter and she was invaluable to her mother while he was away working. The loss of her labor would cause great hardship to Martha.

For the Shona, marriage is a process. There is no particular point when two people suddenly become married. The main purpose of marriage, the Shona believe, is the procreation of children, so a man is permitted to sleep with his wife-to-be before they have become accepted as a married couple. If she proves infertile, he is fully within his rights to return her to her family and either be repaid his bride-price or be given another daughter as a wife. If it can be proven that the man is sterile, it is shameful but not disastrous: He can discreetly arrange for someone else to impregnate the woman. The child that is then born is considered his own.

The government has outlawed polygamy but it still occurs, although most men can afford only one wife. Divorce, however, is quite common. A man can divorce a woman if she is infertile or if she does not fulfill her obligations as a wife. Serious failure as a housewife, repeated infidelity, and the practice of witchcraft can all lead to a woman being sent back to her family by her disgruntled husband. While it is harder for a woman to divorce her husband, it is possible if she can produce evidence of physical abuse or if he fails to keep up his bride-price payments.

Urban Life

That afternoon, as Tafara hoed between the rows of corn, she thought about her future. She was a little frightened of going to live on the cooperative even though it was so close to her family. It was not at all like the life she had known, especially since many of the women there were also ex-freedom fighters and saw themselves as equal to the men. The few she had met scoffed at the old ways, and Tafara knew several had teased Chipo mercilessly for agreeing to pay the bride-price. "This is a cooperative," they reminded him. "If you buy a wife, that means she belongs to us, too."

When Tafara had seen Chipo that morning, she had confessed her fears. Laughing, he had promised that if she was unhappy, he would take her away to Harare where she would have her own house. Tafara didn't like to say it, but that suggestion alarmed her even more. Instead of being enveloped in the great, warm security blanket that is the traditional Shona family, Tafara would be living among strangers whose town ways were totally alien to her. Her concerns are shared by many Shona who find themselves leaving their familiar rural villages for the city.

Perhaps the most fundamental change brought about by urban living is a breakdown of the traditional family structure with its complex web of responsibilities and expectations. Most city dwellers are forced to live in cramped circumstances, making it impossible to maintain an extended family. The position of women is very precarious. Generally, a woman who is seen in a public place is assumed to be a prostitute, which means that wives are often left at home when their husbands go out for

After a visit to the hairdresser, this young resident Harare shows off her "do." Tessa Colvin

Language

Shona, or Chishona as the language is more correctly called, describes a number of closely related dialects. They include: Chikorekore, Chikaranga, Chimanyika, Chindau, and Chizezuru. In the cities, where many *vashona* have come together, a new dialect that also includes many English words has grown up. This is known as *chitaundi*, the language of the town.

*Chi*shona, *Chi*korere, *Chi*karanga: In each of these there is a stem word—the name of the clan—and the prefix *Chi*, which has a function similar to the English suffix "ese," meaning language. Similarly, *Va*shona uses the clan stem word and *Va* to form "the Shona people," and *Mu*shona means "a Shona person." This use of stem words with prefixes, as opposed to the suffixes we are used to in English, is a common characteristic of many Bantu languages—for example, *Si*ndebele is the language of the *Am*andebele, the Ndebele people. Verbs too are constructed with prefixes rather than changing endings.

As in English, there are five vowels in Shona (which is the commonly accepted way of referring both to the people and their language); but whereas in English there are several ways of pronouncing each vowel, in Shona, there is only one pronunciation for each:

a = ah (as in part)
e = eh (as in yet)
i = ee (as in machine)
o = oh (as in short)
u = oo (as in loose)

These are some Shona words: *mukaka* (milk), *masere* (eight), *ini* (I), *musoro* (head), *mukuyu* (fig tree).

Consonants are pronounced the same as in English.

Sindebele has many of the same rules as Chishona, but its vocabulary is different and, because it is a close relative of Zulu, it has click sounds. These are particularly difficult for people who speak languages without clicks to pronounce.

There are three kinds of click in Ndebele (which, like Shona, has come to denote the language and the people).

The dental click, which is written as "c," is pronounced "tsk" (the sound of disapproval): *icansi* (mat), *cela* (ask for), *cina* (end).

The palatal click, written as "q," sounds like a cork popping out of a bottle, *qaphela!* (Look out!).

The lateral click, written as "x," is similar to the cluck used to spur on a horse: *xabana* (quarrel) and *ixuku* (crowd).

ENGLISH	SHONA	NDEBELE
Good morning	Mangwanani	Livuke njani?
Good afternoon	Masikati	Litshonile
Good evening	Manheru	Litshone njani?
How are you?	Makadii zvenyu?	Linjani?
Very well	Ndiripo zvangu	Sikhona
Thank you	Ndatenda	Ngiyabonga
Please	Ndapota	Uxolo
Good-bye	Chisarai zvakanaka	Lisale sesihamba

an evening. This leaves the women isolated not only from their kin, but also from their husbands.

Children born in the cities are liable to grow up ignorant of many of the traditional customs. When they are taken "home" to the country to visit relatives, they often feel superior to these "yokels," and frequently don't know how to behave correctly, particularly toward their elders. Some urban families try to remedy this by sending their children to live for a while with country kin.

Urban Shona often turn to various new types of associations to help overcome the loss of their traditional life. Women join women's clubs in which they give each other help in running their homes. Many men join soccer clubs and some join burial societies which, along with giving members a proper funeral when the time comes, also provide social activities. Churches, youth clubs, charitable organizations, and workers' unions all help to bridge the gap from the old life to the new.

Over time, a new class structure has grown up in the cities to replace the traditional structure based on age, kinship, and hereditary status. At the upper end of the scale are those who have been educated for long periods in Western-style schools and have adopted Western customs and values. This is the new middle class, which occupies the formerly white suburbs. The men, often doctors, lawyers, and government bureaucrats, tend to marry more educated, relatively emancipated women and live a life-style that would be very familiar to most Americans. Sometimes they speak English rather than Shona when they meet and often they have Shona servants.

Food

It is late in the afternoon when Tafara, tired and hungry, returns to the homestead. As she walks along the well-worn path, Tafara stops to pick up firewood whenever she sees a stick. She sees Tichagwa, her fifteen-year-old brother, but she knows he won't help her. At present he is enjoying his status as an adolescent male. Although Tichagwa does not yet have all the privileges of a grown man, Tafara is no longer permitted to boss him around, and each night she brings him his food as he sits with the adult men in the *dare*.

Tafara always knows she is near home when she hears the familiar sounds of women singing and the rhythmic *thump-thump* of the hard *mukonono* pole hitting the softer wood of the *mukuyu* stamping block. It is with this large pestle and mortar that the women grind their grain. Tafara is particularly fond of the *jakwara* (work) songs sung by men and women when they are threshing millet in the winter. They are always very insulting:

> *Have you trouble? What kind of trouble?*
> *Beer is your trouble.*
> *Why can't you leave some for others?*
> *You'd better leave it and go back to your house.*

The women welcome Tafara when they see her. They nod approvingly when they see she has brought some *mowa* leaves, wild amaranthus, which she picked from a bush growing in the rich soil of a former cattle pen. Fatima will boil the leaves and then mix them with homemade peanut butter. This *usavi*, or relish, is eaten with *sadza*. Fatima has also prepared some pumpkin leaves, boiled and left to cool.

When it is time to eat, the men seat themselves in the *dare*, and the women bring them each a bowl of water with which to wash their hands. The older men sit on stones, but Tichagwa and the other teenagers must sit on the ground with their legs crossed. Each man claps quickly and then starts eating. The women wait until the men finish before they eat.

It is dark when everyone has finished. While the younger men sit in the *dare* talking about their day's adventures, the women wash the

Traditional Shona Food

The standard meal of the Shona includes *sadza* (corn porridge) and *usavi* (relish). The *usavi* might be made of a variety of vegetables, fruits, nuts, wild plants, and insects. Meat and fish are eaten less often. Several varieties of mice, including gerbils, are trapped by women and either boiled and dried or grilled on the end of a stick. Wild birds are also eaten. Beef and chicken are eaten on special occasions.

Cultivated vegetables and fruits:
Millet, sorghum, corn, rice, sweet sorghum, cowpeas, peanuts, sweet potatoes, pumpkins, cassava, watermelons, bananas, red peppers, and pineapples.

Wild vegetables and fruits:
The leaves and fruits from a wide variety of indigenous plants are eaten. Particularly savored is the fruit of the baobab tree, which produces a huge pod containing seeds embedded in a white powdery substance. The seeds are sucked and discarded.

Insects:
Locusts: After a swarm has descended, the men and women go to the fields while it is still dark. The sleeping locusts, which have settled on trees and bushes, can be gathered in handfuls. Back at the village, the locusts are poured into a big pot of boiling water and, when cooked, allowed to cool. They are then laid out to dry for a day or two and stored for when a housewife wants to cook up a batch for dinner. Locusts and other insects, being high in protein, replace the meat dish usually found in the Western diet.

Flying Ants: Swarms of flying ants emerge in the summer at the beginning of the rains. To gather them, men insert a small clay pot with a hole in the bottom in the side of an anthill. All other exits from the anthill are then blocked. When the flying ants emerge, they simply walk out through the pot into the waiting hands of the women and children. The women then remove their wings and grill them.

Caterpillars: The type of caterpillars eaten live on the bark and leaves of specific trees. When they are full grown, they are picked off the trees and put through a wringer to squeeze out their intestines. Then they are washed and cooked with a little water. They can be dried and kept throughout the year. Some taste particularly good with peanut butter.

A Shona Dinner: Sadza

                  Usavi—Locusts

                        Pumpkin leaves

Sadza	Place a pot of water on a fire. When it is warm, add a little cornmeal and stir until there are no lumps. Keep on adding meal until the mixture thickens. It should be thick enough to handle easily. Spoon onto plates.
Locusts	Place locusts in a piece of burned clay pot or frying pan. Add a little water and salt and keep stirring them until the water has completely boiled away and the locusts are dry.
Pumpkin Leaves	Cut up leaves, boil until tender, and eat cold.

dishes and get the children ready for bed. Tafara regrets not having had time to go for a swim in the river to wash herself. Instead, after undressing, she pours a small bowl of water and carefully wipes her body with a rag. When she is finished, she stretches out on her mat to rest. Through the doorway, she can see the night sky, aglow with stars. It is a beautiful sight, but as she closes her eyes Tafara sends up her usual prayer for rain. Beauty does not feed empty stomachs.

Voices
of the People

I have striven to make friends with the broken stone
Prayed in the dust of long-forgotten ancestors—
The answer trailed along the falling wall
And disappeared into the dust trodden by unfamiliar feet.
I was led into the scene—
Broken pottery, some gold and beads, the bird made out of stone
All these contained, framed and finally put in the glass case
A quaint scene to excite the imagination of a traveller passing by
But a heap of confusing joy to crush my heart
Against the unresponsive walls.
I have striven to meet morning dancing njuzu

By the spring grandmother had told me about
Wishing to be taken down through the mud
To the world of kind magicians.
I have not seen the njuzu
Neither have I spent my time with them
I am no magician.
I am only a fire side sitter clothed by the dark night
I fear the lion and the leopard will come
Wielding my broken assegai
The only possession recovered from a lost battle
I have woven myself a protective shroud of silence
In preparation for my funeral
I will not forget because there is nothing to forget—
Only this yawning vacancy of nothingness.

These lines from Kizito Muchemwa's poem "The Legacy" eloquently express the struggle of Zimbabwe's people to recapture their past after ninety years of cultural (as well as political) domination by the white colonizers. It is a struggle that reflects the challenge of modern-day Zimbabwe, in which the people are trying to link who they are now with who they were before the onslaught of European education, religion, and attitudes. In their poetry and prose, their sculpture and music, Zimbabweans are rediscovering their cultural past and redefining it in a rich new identity.

Traditional Poetry and Folktales

The Shona have a long tradition of poetry in which they express their joys and sorrows, their relations with each other, and their experiences. These poems are usually sung to the accompaniment of drums, the *mbira* (an African thumb piano), and other traditional instruments, and often consist of a set chorus and verses that are made up on the spot by the lead singer. There are work songs for when the people thresh millet, harvest their crops, or grind their grain; dance songs for parties; spirit songs that mediums dance to; war songs and chants; children's poetry (rather like nursery rhymes), and praise poetry.

Praise poetry, which is rapidly dying out, has a very special place in the cultural history of Zimbabwe's people. It was a medium that they shared with all Bantu peoples. Through these formalized "praises," they expressed their homage to their chiefs, their appreciation for their sweethearts, spouses, and other family members, and their thanks to those who performed certain highly regarded services to their communities.

On the most formal level were those praise poems associated with rulers and religious figures; and on a more personal level there were the clan praises, which often contained references to the sexual attractiveness of its members: the men's hunting skills, the women's chasteness and other virtues that enhanced their marriageability. The ancestral spirits were often invoked in these poems because the Shona believed that it was they, not the actual living individuals, who were responsible for any good a person might do. Wives would recite the "praise names" of their husbands and his ancestors when the men brought home meat from the hunt. Even in lullabies that mothers sang to quiet their crying babies, the words were frequently addressed to the ancestors rather than to the child itself.

Formal praise poems were usually sung in the *dare*, but others were sung in the fields during work or by the women in the village within earshot of the *dare*. These would often be of an insulting nature. Sometimes women would use the opportunity to raise a complaint against their mothers-in-law, or those who thought themselves victims of witch-

An Eye-witness Account, Written by the Portuguese Missionary Father João dos Santos, in 1609 of How Praise Poetry Was Used at the Court of the Shona King Quiteve

The king has another class of people, who are called marombes, *which means the same as jester. These also go round and round the royal dwelling, shouting in very harsh voices many songs and discourses in praise of the king, in the course of which they call him lord of the sun and moon, king of the land and of the rivers, conqueror of his enemies, great in all things, great thief, great wizard, great lion; and all other forms of greatness which they can invent, either good or bad, are attributed to him by them. When the king goes out he is surrounded and encircled by these* marombes, *who recite these praises to him with loud cries, to the sound of small drums, iron and bells, which help them to make a louder noise and clamour. Quiteve also makes use of another class of people, great musicians and dancers, who have no other office than to sit at the first room of the king's palace at the outer door, and round his dwelling, playing many different musical instruments and singing to them a great variety of songs and discourses in praise of the king, in high and sonorous voices.*

craft would let the village (and the suspected witch) know about it through a song.

During courtship, Shona men frequently sang love poems not just to their sweethearts but also in front of other men to boast of their lovers'

A Lullaby

Ru-u, ru-u, ru-u, ru-u.
Haruruhwe, the child is crying.
Haruruhwe, the child is crying.
E, e, e, e, I've heard your complaint, father.
What has been done to you, my father?
How has your child offended you?

E, e, e, e, your complaint has been heard, father-in-law.
What wrong have I, an outsider, done?
Why, I came here for your service.
If there is something wrong, let it be stated and
requited.

Be quiet now, Matendera!
Be quiet now, Zvimbakupa!
Be quiet now, Zomba!
You vaHota are chiefs without question.
Hunting and the chase is your right here.
The soil and the rubbish on it is all yours.

Let me, your child, have some rest as well.
I must have done something terrible today.
Calm yourself, my father.
I am repentant. I won't do so again.
Lay me down upon the ground and let me rest.
My legs are stiff from standing since I came.

In this lullaby, the mother invokes her own father, then her husband's father, and then the spirits of his clan. She asks them all what she has done for them to make her child cry. They should be magnanimous, she says, because they are chiefs. Finally, she appeals once more to her father since her appeals to the husband's spirits have been to no avail.

attributes. This had the social function of allowing a man to express the seriousness of his romantic intentions in front of the whole village. At beer drinks, husbands tried to outdo each other in their praises about their wives and mothers. These poems were less formal, allowing the speaker some creativity in making up lines applicable to the person to whom the poem applied. They were often lighthearted and humorous as well.

One way the Shona transmit their culture and its rules to their children is through folktales. In the past these tales were always told on autumn and winter evenings after the crops had been harvested and there was no more work to do. To tell a folktale during the daytime or in the busy summer was seen as a breach of the spirit of the stories, which were designed to teach children as well as entertain them. These tales are very much like Aesop's fables in that they always have a moral. For example, in one, a group of sisters are persuaded by some smooth-talking young men to elope, rather than go through the traditional drawn-out marriage process. Later, the men are transformed into lions and the foolish young women are only saved by their wiser younger brother. The moral of the story is that a young woman must closely examine the family into which she marries because she will have to live with them.

Many folktales have animals as the characters. These animals symbolize certain vices and virtues. The hare, intelligent and quick, is often the hero. The baboon, vain and stupid, is frequently the one who is outwitted.

Modern Literature

In the last few decades, Zimbabweans, influenced by the work of European and American writers, have begun to pioneer a new form of

In Praise of a Mother

You are my mother, One with loving embraces,
 One with a neck long as a giraffe's.
 You cooked bean stew for the chief,
 And he forgot to judge the case at court.
One full of grateful praise,
 You praised the chief at the field,
 And there came a drizzle of rain outside.
My mother, One who stays behind to care for others,
 You stayed to brighten even the contented.
 You said, "Come and let me praise you,"
 But then you went on to praise a frog,
 So that it burnt a pot of bean stew at its mother-in-law's.
 My calabash, so light yet so capacious.
 Tasty paste that sticks to my gums,
 Ground nuts doubly ground.
My mother who cares for orphans,
 You show pity,
 And beauty like a calf grazing towards cowhood.
One whose company is a delight,
 You comforted the weaned child,
 And it thought, "Here is peace at last." The dead never saw the
  like.

literature, written in the vernacular (the local languages). These poems, novels, plays, and short stories incorporate many of the characteristics of European literature while expressing the African cultural and philosophical outlook. This makes them very difficult to translate into English because the Shona and Ndebele languages make use of ideophones, which are words, impossible to express in English, that indicate an action or manner of action, a state, a color, a sound, a smell or a sensation. For example, the literal translation of *Kudoti pasi go, nde-e nazvo tuzu* would be: "Then down on the ground—go, *nde-e tuzu*—as a result of that." To make sense of it, the translator has to find as close a meaning as possible. In this case, it might be: "Then it sat on the ground, just looking, at a loss for what to do as a result of this."

African languages are rooted in the concrete, day-to-day world and are extremely graphic and picturesque. Even in their everyday conversations, Africans prefer to express themselves in metaphors. For example, an aunt speaking to her brother about her niece who has become pregnant for the first time might say, "The child has stepped on the moon," meaning the child is no longer having her monthly period. The father might then reply, "Whose was the bull that broke into my cattle *kraal*?" This love of imagery is carried over to Shona literature.

Some black Zimbabweans also write in English, and there are several white writers who have recorded the white experience in Zimbabwe. The most famous of these is Doris Lessing, who grew up in the Southern Rhodesia of the 1930's and 1940's, and cast an unflinching eye on the master-servant relationship between whites and blacks.

Among the best black writers are Solomon Mutswairo and Charles Mungoshi, who have written prose and poetry in both English and Shona. Mutswairo is best known for his novels *Feso* and, more recently, *Mapondera: Soldier of Zimbabwe.* In this latter book he tells the true story of a man who lived, fought, and died in the period of about 1840 to 1907 in the Mazowe area of Zimbabwe. It is a celebration of the life of the Rozvi in the years just before and during the white settlement of the country.

Mungoshi's novels *Waiting for the Rain* and *Coming of the Dry Season* are about the situation of the modern-day Shona. This situation is best expressed in his words:

> *Poised on the thin edge of now*
> *like a poleaxed tightrope walker*
> *the past a roaring lion in the underbrush*
> *the future a nuclear mushroom I can't swallow.*

Since the civil war, there has been an outpouring of plays, poems, and novels in which Zimbabweans, black and white, have expressed their feelings about this tragic period in the country's history.

Shona Sculpture

A thousand years ago the sculptors of Great Zimbabwe carved the soapstone birds that linked the inhabitants of the city to the heavens above. They also etched symbolic geometric designs on great monoliths (blocks of stones). Then, somewhere between that long-ago age and the twentieth century, the art of sculpting was completely lost. All that remained were the wood carvers, *muvezi*, who were held in high regard by the Shona. But they no longer used their skill purely to express religious ideas or symbols. Instead they concerned themselves with the things of this world: wooden plates, mortars, pestles, hoes, spears, drums, and headrests.

Two Poems Written in the Aftermath of the War

ZIMBABWE

by Gloria Sibanda

Zimbabwe where were you Zimbabwe?
Our Motherland.
People were crying for you.
People died for you.
Others are cripples because of you Zimbabwe.
Others lost their families because of you.
People suffered for many years because of you.
You were nowhere to be found.
Where were you?
Blood was shed like rain.
Others were living in the mountains.
Where were you all along?
What kind of punishment is that?
Our beloved Motherland.
You came back later after we suffered.
We have brought you back.
People are happy now.
They unite because of you.
Because of the blood of those who died for you.
Motherland Zimbabwe you are back.

RHODESIAN LULLABY
by John Eppel

Like shrapnel from an old bomb we scatter
to other lands, delivering reasons.
On our elbows and our knees, a season's
grass-burns. On the backs of our hands, faces,
and necks—the first traces of skin cancer.
Yes, we're Rhodesians. Does it matter?

Even our children have learned not to cry
for their puppies' graves. The women weep
no more for their gardens. And the men sleep
less fitfully on their way to Smithland
or Salisbury-by-the-sea. A boozy band
of rebels, we fought the world and lost. Why

should it matter? Rhodesians never die.
From our mouths flat patriotisms slide
tight as trouser-legs, unbending as pride.
Stories of war spread like phosphorus
to our eyes. In a trickling of pus
and blood down cheeks, we shout our lullaby.

Our wallets were fat, our bellies fatter.
Memories of war slip like envelopes
under the doors of our minds. Each one copes
in his own way—a defiant slogan
on a T-shirt, the old flag printed on
a dish-cloth . . . hush now—it doesn't matter.

A Shona sculptor and some of his creations. Zimbabwe Ministry of Information

The 1960's was to see a revival of sculpting among the Shona, thanks largely to a white man, Frank McEwen, who was the first director of what was then Rhodesia's National Gallery of Art. McEwen was determined to inspire the Shona to once more return to the stonework of their past. He deliberately offered no formal art classes, fearful that the Shona artists would be influenced by European ideas. Instead, he merely provided sculpture materials and equipment, and persuaded the new sculptors to work from their imaginations, drawing on the rich Shona background of traditional folklore and religion. The result was

Tengenenge Sculpture Community

At Tengenenge Farm one can always depend on hearing two sounds. One is the singing of the cicadas; the other is the light *chink chink* of chisels hitting stone. In the shade of the mahobohobo trees, men in coveralls crouch over their labors. Around them is a whole cast of characters that have sprung from the creative Shona mind. Most are deceptively simple and stylized: a water bird, its long graceful neck conveying the very essence of the creature; a dramatic figure, as abstract as a Picasso, but as African as its creator.

This "farm" is, as Tengenenge's founder puts it, "a divine accident." He is Tom Blomefield, a former tobacco farmer and big game hunter who, in the mid-1960's, decided to give up farming and try sculpting. He was in the right place. His farm was situated on the Great Dyke, which offered great quantities of high quality stone. Blomefield invited his black farm laborers to join him in this interesting new experiment. Among them was a carver, Crispin Chakonyoka, who gave one piece of advice to the enthusiasts: "Start at the head and work down." It was the only art lesson most of them ever had.

Before long, Blomefield was selling the work of the Tengenenge artists in Harare and would-be sculptors were arriving daily to join the community. Each was given a set of chisels and told to pick out a spot under the trees and not copy anyone else. To smooth over fears the conservative rural Africans had that such a novel activity might displease the spirits, gifts were sent to the local mediums to keep the ancestors happy.

Tengenenge had to be closed down for a while during the war when the area became too dangerous. Blomefield sold the farm but kept the rights to fifteen acres, where there is a good supply of stone. He reopened the community when peace returned.

an outpouring of a new kind of African sculpture that was named the Workshop School. In other parts of the country, other whites provided the same kind of impetus for local Shona artists.

Today Shona sculptures are known throughout the world. The work of men like Henry Munyaradzi, Bernard Matemera, and Nicholas Mukomberanwa have been exhibited at New York's Museum of Modern Art, the Rodin Museum in Paris, and in Los Angeles, London, and Sydney. The sculptors' creative source remains the folklore, religion, and mythology of traditional life. A large percentage of their work is based on animals, which usually represent the moral or ethical qualities they have in Shona folklore.

Modern-day Shona sculptors have abandoned the soapstone used by the artists of Great Zimbabwe because it is too soft and fragile. Instead, they now work in the harder serpentines and granites found in many places around the country. These stones come in blacks, grays, and browns as well as shades of green, deep red, and purple. The sculptures are unique, being neither traditionally African nor European. They are reminiscent of the stylized Zimbabwe birds, yet they have a feeling, too, of today. Some are huge and powerful, others peaceful and serene. And even though most Americans and Europeans do not understand the Shona imagination from which they sprang, the sculptures still impart a universal message that is understood by all.

Music and Dance

Music provides the backdrop to much of the life of Zimbabwe. In the country the people often sing as they work, and dancing is used both for enjoyment and as part of numerous rituals including spirit possession. The style is flamboyant and the *manyawi* (the spirit of the dancers) dictates the pace of the tune. Although many of the dances are centuries

Traditional dancing is no longer limited to the village. In the cities people join clubs and sometimes take part in competitions. Tessa Colvin

Practice session for a young band.   Tessa Colvin

old, Zimbabweans also use the medium of traditional dance to re-create scenes from more recent history—for example, the colonial takeover of the country, the war, and independence. Traditional musicians, usually a drummer and an *mbira* player, are in great demand. The tunes tend to be simple and repetitive, with importance being laid on the rhythm rather than the melody.

Drums are made in a variety of sizes to provide different pitches and are usually carved from solid blocks of wood. The sound of the handheld *mbira*, or thumb piano, is produced when flat iron tines, fixed to a wooden soundboard, are plucked with the thumb. Another popular instrument is the *marimba*, which is very similar to the xylophone.

In the city, the music one usually hears booms from shop doors, open car windows, and handheld radios. Here one is more likely to hear reggae or the *kwela* music (a modern African-Western hybrid) that originated in the townships of South Africa. Reggae is very popular in Zimbabwe. The late Bob Marley appeared at Zimbabwe's independence ceremonies in 1980.

Today's Zimbabwean musicians often include a political message in their songs, usually to show solidarity with South Africa's blacks who are still suffering under that country's policy of racial segregation. In 1987 the American musician Paul Simon chose Harare as the site for his Graceland concert, which brought together musicians from a number of African countries. The following year one of Zimbabwe's top bands, the Bhundu Boys, went on a world tour that included the United States.

The health of a people is frequently reflected in the health of its cultural life. The outpouring of creativity among Zimbabweans bodes well for the country's future. There is a vitality and optimism that transcends the uncertainties of a nation in transition. The people of Zimbabwe understand this well.

> *The sunrise of our country is come,*
> *And our great task is now begun.*
>
> Solomon Mutswairo

Conclusion: Beacon of Hope

Zimbabwe is a country of extraordinary promise. It has rich resources in both its land and its people. It has come through its tumultuous birth to find peace and relative stability. This is no mean achievement on the troubled continent of Africa where ethnic rivalries, failed social experiments, and dictatorships by elites have so often led to no improvement in the lives of the people who had hoped for so much when their countries struggled from beneath the yoke of colonialism. In its short life, Zimbabwe has become a leader and a beacon to many of these countries. Its continued prosperity sustains them both materially and spiritually.

For Zimbabweans themselves, the future contains hope, despite some of the problems the country has struggled with since independence. Material wealth has not come to everyone, and certainly there are those who are disappointed by the undramatic nature of the country's revolution. Yet the great majority of the people believe they are better off today than they were in 1980. More importantly, they feel they have the opportunity to improve their lives. They have acquired that very American right to pursue happiness.

Joshua Pongweni is a very old man now. As he sits in a dusty armchair outside his hut in the evening, watching the sun slip behind the western hills, he sometimes mistakes the cry of the nightjar for the voices of his forefathers calling to him. They seem very close now and

A village elder keeps his young audience enthralled with folktales. For over a thousand years children in Zimbabwe have learned the lessons of their culture in this way. Tessa Colvin

they no longer speak in the faint tones of old men. Instead their voices are strong, those of warriors who stride across the land confident and free.

Joshua longs to join them, but until then he is happy sitting by his hut waiting for his granddaughter to bring him his beer. He is still waiting for the land he hoped for at independence, and his life will probably run out before he gets it. But even that is not so important to Joshua anymore. The leopard licks all its spots, black and white. The government will get around to the Pongweni family eventually. What is important to Joshua is that his father was born in a free country and he himself will die in a free country. Before too many generations have passed, Joshua's life and his father's will merge into one and the period when Zimbabwe was not free will seem very short.

AT SUNSET

Now, the sun goes down,
Night's shadows creep across the land,
Darkness spreads quickly on the earth,
*   As cattle egrets cry out.*

Beneath the last lighted clouds,
Blazing in the lost glaze of light,
The sky suffuses bleeding a crimson spray,
*   At the ends of the earth.*

Listen, what's that stir in the bush?
A flutter, then the crowded birds chorus out,
Perched in branches, pierced by shafts of last sun,
*   Just before night engulfs all things.*

Now, let's turn to the city,
Brash street lights blaze (no need of sun)
Sparkling like blown-up diamonds—
  Light balloons, rivals of the stars above.

Beneath them, among the people of the city,
Never sleeping in all its parts,
Man and woman brighten their lives with money—
  Electric, golden, their earthly deceits.

Listen, hear the city's shouts and curses:
Manwomanchild and machines grind out a howl,
Dark streets, garish-streaked by neon,
  Fight the night, sleep is defeated.

When the country sun goes down,
Troubled minds find rest, get rest,
Their peace is dream their sleep unbroken,
  No city clamour; country man snores unwoken.

Solomon Mutswairo

Bibliography

Print Resources

There is little good material available on Zimbabwe in most local libraries in the United States. What can be found is frequently out of date, reflects the prejudices of the colonial era, or is even, alas, fraught with inaccuracies. Readers wanting to expand their knowledge of the country will have to search beyond their neighborhoods.

The Library of Congress in Washington, D.C., has a fine collection of books on every aspect of the country. Libraries at larger colleges and in big cities might also be a good place to look. Failing access to any of these, the interested reader will have to order books directly from publishers in Zimbabwe and the United States. The names and addresses of these are included at the end of this section.

General Books

Carr, Archie. *The Land and Wildlife of Africa.* Alexandria, Va: Time-Life Books, 1980. This book, available in most libraries, provides a good general description of the geography of Africa and the animals that live there. There is a particularly fine section (Chapter 5) about the relationship between the savanna and Africa's big game. The book also addresses some of the ecological problems that face African countries.

Nelson, Harold D. *Zimbabwe, A Country Study.* Washington, D.C.: United States Government, 1983.

This is part of a series of country studies put out by the U.S. Government and sold in government bookstores. Although a little dry, it provides a good, fairly detailed account of Zimbabwe's history, geography, economy, and government. Written before the country became a one-party state, its government and politics section is now out of date.

Mazrui, Ali A. *The Africans, A Triple Heritage.* Boston: Little, Brown, 1986.

Based on the Public Broadcasting System television series, this book provides a provocative view of modern Africa as seen through the eyes of an African. It is of particular interest to readers who wish to understand the many forces—traditionalism, imperialism, and capitalism—that have contributed to the context within which Zimbabwe exists. This book is widely available throughout the United States.

History

July, Robert W. *A History of the African People.* New York: Scribners, 1974.

Curtin, Philip; Steven Feierman; Leonard Thompson; and Jan Vansina. *African History.* Boston: Little, Brown, 1978.

Oliver, Roland, and J. D. Fage. *A Short History of Africa.* New York: Penguin, 1977.

All three of these books provide good straightforward accounts of the migrations and history of the Bantu, including the Shona and Ndebele. They also address the period of colonization and decolonization, although all were written before independence in Zimbabwe. They are useful in setting the history of Zimbabwe within the context of African history as a whole.

Beach, D. N. *The Shona and Zimbabwe, 900–1850.* New York: Africana Publishing Co., 1980.

———. *War and Politics in Zimbabwe, 1840–1900.* Gweru, Zimbabwe: Mambo Press, 1986.

Prof. David Beach is one of the best authorities on the Shona and their past, and both these books are indispensable to a deeper understanding of the Shona people. They are, however, difficult to read and understand.

Garlake, Peter S. *The Great Zimbabwe.* New York: Stein & Day, 1973.

———. *Life at Great Zimbabwe.* Gweru, Zimbabwe: Mambo Press, 1983.

These are the best accounts of the building and culture of Great Zimbabwe by one of the country's leading authorities on the ruined city. The second book is for younger readers.

Rasmussen, R. Kent. *Mzilikazi of the Ndebele.* London: Heinemann Educational, 1977.

This is a good short biography of Mzilikazi and his search for a homeland.

Bhebe, Ngwabi. *Lobengula of Zimbabwe.* London: Heinemann Educational, 1977.

Written by an Ndebele, this book paints a sympathetic portrait of Lobengula and his times.

Mason, Philip. *The Birth of a Dilemma: the Conquest and Settlement of Rhodesia.* London: Oxford University Press, 1958.

Although old, this book gives a balanced and highly readable account of the influence of white settlement of Zimbabwe.

Meredith, Martin. *The Past Is Another Country: Rhodesia 1890–1979.* London: Andre Deutsch, 1979

A highly readable account of the period of white colonization of Zimbabwe.

Raeburn, Michael. *We Are Everywhere: Narratives from Rhodesian Guerrillas.* New York: Random House, 1979.

For those interested in reading a lively account of the lives of those who fought for black independence, this is a must. It gives a good idea of the dangers, difficulties, and thinking of the guerrillas.

Caute, David. *Under the Skin: The Death of White Rhodesia.* London: Allen Lane, 1983.

Invaluable for those wanting to learn more about the fears and motivations of white Rhodesians. This is Caute's first-person account of his experiences in Zimbabwe in the years just before independence.

Martin, David, and Phyllis Johnson. *The Struggle for Zimbabwe: The Chimurenga War.* Boston: Faber & Faber, 1981.

Gann, Lewis H., and Thomas H. Henrikson. *The Struggle for Zimbabwe: Battle in the Bush.* New York: Praeger, 1981.

These two books give different views of the civil war, the first from the side of the guerrillas, the second from the side of the government forces. Read together, they give a balanced view of the conflict.

There are also a number of fascinating accounts by missionaries and explorers of the country before colonization. Of particular interest are *Sunshine and Storm in Rhodesia*, by Frederick Courteney Selous, and Robert Moffat's *Matabele Journals, 1829–1860.*

Politics, Government, and Economy

Those interested in reading more about Zimbabwe's modern politics and economy will have to rely on magazine and newspaper accounts, because little has been written since independence about these aspects of the country. *The New York Times* and *The Christian Science Monitor* (both indexed) are particularly useful.

Customs, Art, and Culture

Bourdillon, Michael F. C. *The Shona Peoples: An Ethnography of the Contemporary Shona with Special Reference to Their Religion.* Gweru, Zimbabwe: Mambo Press, 1976.

   An excellent account of the customs, culture, and religion of the Shona. Despite the daunting title, it is also easy to read.

Weiss, Ruth. *The Women of Zimbabwe.* London: Kesho Publications, 1986.

   This book, which relies heavily on first-person accounts, provides an accurate view of the lot of Zimbabwean women today.

Arnold, Marion I. *Zimbabwean Stone Sculpture.* Bulawayo, Zimbabwe: Louis Bolze, 1986.

   Although scholarly, this is the best book on Shona sculpture available today. It also includes some excellent photographs.

Ellert, H. *The Material Culture of Zimbabwe.* Harare, Zimbabwe: Longman Zimbabwe, 1984.

   A good account of the crafts, musical instruments, and tools of Zimbabwe's people.

To obtain novels, poetry, and plays by Zimbabwean writers, it is suggested that readers send for catalogs from these publishing houses:

Three Continents Press
1638 Connecticut Avenue, NW
Washington, D.C. 20009

The Red Sea Press, Inc.
556 Bellevue Avenue
Trenton, N.J. 08618

Africa World Press, Inc.
P.O. Box 1892
Trenton, N.J. 08607

Zimbabwe Publishing House
P.O. Box 350
Harare
Zimbabwe

Mambo Press
P.O. Box 779
Gweru
Zimbabwe

The Poetry Society of Zimbabwe
P.O. Box A70
Avondale
Harare
Zimbabwe

Books of Zimbabwe
P.O. Box 1994
Bulawayo
Zimbabwe

Longman Zimbabwe
Tourle Rd
Ardbennie
Harare
Zimbabwe

Discography

These are examples of the variety of Zimbabwean recordings available in the United States:

Album Title	Artist(s)	Record Label and Catalog Number
The Chimurenga Singles	Thomas Mapfumo	Earthworks (ELP 2004)
Shabini	The Bhundu Boys	Discafrique (AFRI LP 02)
Viva Zimbabwe:		
Dance Music of Zimbabwe	Various	Carthage (CGLP 4411)
Amandla!	Lovemore Majaivana and the Zulu Band	ZIM (003)
Shona Mbira Music	Various	Nonesuch (H 72077)
Master of Mbira from Zimbabwe	Ephat Mujuru	Lyrichord (LLST 7398)

Filmography

Moving On: The Hunger for Land in Zimbabwe
Peter Entell, 1982
52 minutes
Southern Africa Media Center

A sensitive portrayal of the problems of land allocation in Zimbabwe. The contrasting stories of the black Chifamba family and the white King family highlight the difficulties the Zimbabwean government faces in balancing the aspirations of the peasants with the need to keep the country's economy viable.

After the Hunger and the Drought
Ollie Maruma, 1988.
54 minutes
Southern Africa Media Center

Leading Zimbabwean writers and intellectuals discuss the difficulties of finding a new identity in an independent Zimbabwe. The issue of traditionalism versus modern Western life and thought is especially highlighted.

Corridors of Freedom
Simon Bright, 1987
52 minutes
Southern Africa Media Center
  This film chronicles the story of how Zimbabwe and other black African countries
  became dependent on white-ruled South Africa, and how they are now attempting
  to break that bond. The efforts of the Southern African Development Coordination
  Conference (SADCC) are highlighted.
Destructive Engagement
Toni Stasburg, 1987
52 minutes
Southern Africa Media Center
  This film graphically depicts South Africa's campaign of destabilization against
  Zimbabwe and its black neighbors.
No Easy Walk
Bernard Odjijda, 1988
3 parts, 60 minutes each
The Cinema Guild
  This three-part series studies the history of colonialism and the struggles for
  independence of three countries. Part One deals with Ethiopia, part two with Kenya,
  and part three with Zimbabwe. Odjijda contrasts black and white versions of events.
  The section on Zimbabwe includes interviews with Robert Mugabe, Joshua Nkomo,
  Ian Smith, and other Zimbabweans.
Nkuleleko Means Freedom
Ron and Ophera Hallis, 1982.
28 minutes
First Run/Icarus Films
  A portrayal of Zimbabwe's new educational system that strives to combine teaching
  practical skills with modern traditional school subjects.
Zimbabwe: The New Struggle
Ron Hallis, 1985
58 minutes
First Run/Icarus Films
  An overview of Zimbabwe in the middle of its first decade of independence, this
  documentary highlights some of the country's most pressing problems.

  For further information and catalogs, write to:
Southern Africa Media Center
630 Natoma Street
San Francisco, Calif. 94103
(415)621–6196

The Cinema Guild
1697 Broadway, Suite 802
New York, N.Y. 10019
(212)246–5522

First Run/Icarus Films
200 Park Avenue South, Suite 1319
New York, N.Y. 10003
(212)674–3375

The National Geographic Society puts out many excellent films and videos on the animal life in Africa. Of special interest are *African Wildlife*, *Lions of the African Night*, and *The Rhino War*.

For the catalog, write to:
National Geographic Society
Educational Services, Department 89
Washington, D.C. 20036

Index

Numbers in *italics* refer to illustrations.

African National Congress (South Africa), 141

African National Council (ANC), 101, 109

Africans. *See* blacks.

agriculture, 19, 29
  cooperatives, 139, 143, 151, *155*, 193, 198
  economy and, 100, 128, 138, 144
  game farming, 157
  peasant farming, 143, 147–51, *149, 150, 179*
  precolonial, 33, 34, 43
  rainy seasons and, 5, 7
  white commercial farming, 5, 13, 128, 138, *138*, 146–49, 178

AIDS (Aquired Immune Deficiency Syndrome), *170*, 177

Air Zimbabwe, 160

ancestral spirits, 2, 36, 38, 43, 82, 148, 172, 174, 183, 185, 186, 190, 193, 209. *See also* religion.

Angola, 22, 162

assegai, 52, 59, 72

"At Sunset" (Mutswairo), 226–27

Baines, Thomas, *60*

Bangala Dam, 29

Bantu, 5, 12, 14, 21, 32, 58
  origins, 34

Bantu Congress, 96

baobab tree, 21, *21*

Barreto, Francisco, 13

beer, 1, 33, 186, 226

Beira Corridor, 141, 162

Bhundu Boys, 223

blacks
  attitude to whites, 67, 123
  under colonialism, 87–90, 105, 106
  colonial legislation affecting, 81, 92, 93
  political movements, 96, 97
  registration, 88, 92

Blomefield, Tom, 219
Botswana, 9, 10, 145, 162
bride-price, 183, 196, 197
British Empire, 67, 68, 70
British government, 94–96, 99, 100, 108,
  121, 123
British settlers, 7, 53, 70, *75*, 78–97
  attitudes toward blacks, 51, 61, 62, 67,
    92
  "Pioneer Column," 69, 74, *75*
British South Africa Company (BSAC), 69,
  72, 74, 78, 80, 83
British South Africa Police (BSAP), 74, 94
Bulawayo, 14, 18, 85, 94, 124, 154, 174
  Lobengula's *kraal* at, 18, 67, 74

Carrington, Lord, 121, 123
cattle, 2, 13, 20, 21, 33, 55, 59, 60, 83,
  144
  traditional role of, 39, 82, 112, 196
Chakonyoka, Crispin, 219
Chaminuka, 2, 30, 39, 185
Changamire (title) 48, 49, 51
Changamire state, 33, 49–51, 55
Chauke, Justin, 116
chidawo, 38
Chihunduru, Torwa, 48
Chikuyo Chisamarengu, Mutapa, 46
Chimanimani Mountains, 17, 19
chimurenga
  first, 82–87
  second, 111–17
"Chimurenga Song", 109
chisi (sacred spirit days), 148
Chitako, 44, 46
Christianity, 67, 87, 188, 189
  missionaries and, *47*, 53, 57, *63*, 64,
    131, 135, 136
cities, 18, 19
  urban life, 198–202
civil war
  government forces and, 115–18, 120
  guerrillas and, 109, *112*, 111–17, 193,
    194
  peasants and, 111–17, 120
  terrorism and, 114, 115
  whites and, 106, 113, 117, *119*, 120

clans, 34
Coghlan, Sir Charles, *91*
colonialism, 67–69, 70, 72, 78–80, 87–92.
  See also British settlers.
  education under, 90, 104
Coming of the Dry Season (Mungoshi), 215
communal lands, 20, 21, 137, 148, 151
communism, 102, 113, 127, 130, 133
conservation of animals, 151, 152–54
Conservative Alliance of Zimbabwe (CAZ),
  105, 130
corn, 10, 13, 138, 143, 147, 151
courts, 180, 181
courtship, 194–97
currency, 145, 146
customary law, 181, 183, 184

da Silveira, Dom Goncalo, 12, *47*
Danangombe, 48
dance, 220, *221*, 222
dare, 2, 203, 209
Declaration of Rights, 140
Dhlodhlo. *See* Danangombe.
dissidents, *128*, 130, 132, 136
divorce, 197
Dombo, Changamire, 33, 49
dwala, 16, 73

Eastern Highlands, 17, 19
economic sanctions, 99–104, 146
economy, 16, 100, 126–28, 142–62
education, 90, 104, 125–26, 163–69, *164*,
  166
elections, 120, 121, *121*, 123, 136. *See
  also* franchise.
Eppel, John, 217
escarpment, *17*, 20

family, 190–93
Federation of Rhodesia and Nyasaland, 81,
  94
Fernandes, Antonio, 33, 46
Feso (Mutswairo), 214
Field, Winston, 81, 95, 97
Fifth Brigade, 134

flame lily, 7
folktales, 212, 225
foreign exchange, 154, 157, 176
forests, 17, 18, 22, 32
franchise, 91, 94, 95, 108. *See also*
    elections.

geology, 15, 16
Ghana, 95, 132
gold, 12, 16, 30, 32, 39, 48, 62, 146
    mining, 40, 46, 49, *50*, 144
government of Zimbabwe, xiii, 125, 130,
    137, 143, 184, 197
    business and, 154, 156, 157
    economy and, 143, 146, 151, 159, 160,
        162
    education and, 163–69, *166*
    health care and, 176
    neighboring states and, 138, 141, 160
    one-party state and, xiii, 136
    whites and, 129, 130, 146, 147
Graceland concert, 223
Great Dyke, 16, 219
Great Zimbabwe, 30–34, *31*, 39–43, *42*,
    215, 220
Guqukani Cooperative, 154
Gwelo. *See* Gweru.
Gweru, 18, 85, 111

H. J. Heinz Co., 156
Harare, *11*, 14, 18, *19*, 105, 123, 142,
    174, 198. *See also* Salisbury.
Hartley, Henry, 62
health care, *170*
    modern, 169, 171, 176–77
    traditional, 171–74
highveld, 10, *10*, 12–15, *17*, 20, 39
Huggins, Sir Godfrey, 80, 81, 91, 93
hut tax, 83
Hwange Game Reserve, 21
hydroelectric power, 28

ideophones, 214
impis, 60, 61
"In Praise of a Mother," 213

independence, 1–4, 101, 121, 123, *129*,
    142, 165
    in Africa, 93, 94, 95, 97
Industrial and Commercial Workers' Union
    (ICU), 96
Industrial Development Corporation (IDC),
    157
industry, 18, 19, 154, 160, 161. *See also*
    manufacturing.
Inyangani, Mount, xii, 17
irrigation, 21, 29

Jacobsen, Mark, 118
jakwana (work) songs, 203
justice, 180–84

Kaguvi, *86*, 87
Karanga, 43, 46
Kariba, Lake, xii, 20, 28
    construction of, 26, *27*
    hydroelectric power and, 28
Kariba Valley, xiii
Katsande, Caroline, 90
Kawere School, 164, 165
Kenya, 13, 93, 94
Khami, 32, 48
Khoisans, 12, 14–16, 32, 34
Kipling, Rudyard, 8, 9, 29
Kissinger, Dr. Henry, 104, 120
kopje, 10, 16, 40, 61, *75*, 78, 85
kraal, 16, *17*, 18, 67, 68, 88

Lancaster House, 101, 121–23, 130
land
    division between blacks and whites, *79*,
        80, 82, 92, 108, 137
    resettlement, 92, 137, 138, 226
Land Apportionment Act (1930), 92,
    108
Land Tenure Act (1969), 100, 101, 108
"Legacy, The" (Muchemwa), 207–8
Legal Age of Majority Act (LAMA), 167,
    168
Lessing, Doris, 214
Limpopo railway, 162

Limpopo River, 9, 22, 28, 34, 49, 57, 59, 62
literature, 208, 212, 214, 215
Livingstone, David, 22
Lobengula, 62–69, *66*, 82, 96
  Bulawayo and, 18, 53, 67
  character of, 76, 77
  Matabele War and, 72, 73
  whites and, 67, 69
lowveld, 10, *17*, 20, 21, 39
"Lullaby, A," 211
Lundi River, xii
Lusaka, 20, 135

Machel, Samora, 126
Macmillan, Harold, 94
malaria, 12, 41, 46
Malawi, 13, 93, 97, 162, 177. *See also* Nyasaland.
Mandela, Nelson, 132
Manicaland, 9
manufacturing, 101, 104, 145, 146, 156, 157, *159*. *See also* industry.
Mapfure College, 168
Mapondera: Soldier of Zimbabwe (Mutswairo), 214
Maputo, 162
marimba (xylophone), 223
marriage customs, 193–97
Marx, Karl, 127, 132
Marxism, 127, 143, 189
Mashonaland, 9, 86, 178, 185
  British settlement of, 53, 62, 67, 68, 69, 74, 80
Masvingo Province, 9
Matabele War, 72, 73
Matabeleland, 9, 83, 134, 154, *155*
  British settlement of, 67–69
  Ndebele establishment of, 53, 60
Matemera, Bernard, 220
Matope, 37
Matopo Hills, 16, 73, 85
  Mwari cave cult and, 87, 187–89
Matusadonha Mountains, 20
Mavuradonha Mountains, 19
mbira (thumb piano), 209, 222, 223
McEwen, Frank, 218

mfecane, 49
mhondoro, 38, 186. *See also* ancestral spirits.
middleveld, 20, 39
Midlands, 9, 18
millet, 1, 144, 186, 204, 209
minerals, 16, 100, 144. *See also* mining.
mining, 18, *50*, 144, 154, *158*, 160. *See also* gold.
Mkwati, 87
Moffat, Dr. Robert, 53, 57, 62, *63*, 64, 65
Monclaro, Father Francisco, 12, 13
mountains, 17–20, 32
Moyo, Elizabeth, 114
Mozambican National Resistance (MNR), 141
Mozambique, 8, 10, 18, 126
  Mutapa state and, 33, 43, 48
  Rhodesian civil war and, 117, 119, 125
  Zimbabwe national security and, 141, 157, 162
Mtilikwe River, 29
Muchemwa, Kizito, 208
mudzimu, 38, 186. *See also* ancestral spirits.
Mugabe, Robert, 97, 101, 117, 121, 125, 143
  "dissidents" and, 130, 132, 133, 136
  character of, 131–33
  socialism and, 126, 132
  South Africa and, 160
  ZANU-PF and, 123, 128, 136, 137
Mugabe, Sally, 132
Mukomberanwa, Nicholas, 220
Mungoshi, Charles, 214, 215
Munhumutapa. *See* Mutapa (title).
Munyaradzi, Henry, 220
music, 208, 209, 220, 221, 222, *222*, 223
Muslim traders, 12, 13, 32
Mutapa (title), 33, 43, 44, *45*, 46, *47*, 48, 49
Mutapa state, 12, 43–48
Mutare, 19, 72, 109–11, *119*
Mutota, 37
Mutswairo, Solomon, 214, 223, 227
mutupo. *See* totems.
Muzorewa, Bishop Abel, 101, 109, 120, 121, 123

Mwari, 49, 51, 148, 187
  cave cult of, 16, 62, 87, 88, 188–90
Mzilikazi, 16, 51, *56*, 52–62, 76, 77
  character of, 64, 65
  military genius of, 58, 59
  Voortrekkers and, 52, 55, 57–59,
   73

n'anga. *See* spirit mediums.
Namibia, 8
National Democratic Party (NDP), 96
National Gallery of Art, 218
nationalism, 96, 97, 104, 111
nationalists, 92, 104, 108, 117, 120,
  131–35
National Railways of Zimbabwe (NRZ),
  18
national security, 138–41
Native reserves, 80, 89
Ndebele, 16, 18, 29, 51, 52–69, *56*, *60*.
  See also dissidents.
  language, 200, 214
  as military nation, 7, 41, 49, 52, 55, 58,
   59
  origins, 55
  political movements, 96, 97
  relationship with Shona, 61, 130, 135,
   136
  uprising against settlers, 82–85
Ndebele Home Society, 96
negotiations, 100, 101, 135
  British government and, 108, 121
  "internal settlement," 120
  United States and, 104, 120
Nehanda, 2, 38, 185
  mediums, 87, 114
Nguni, 49, 51, 55
Nkomo, Joshua, 97, 117, 123
  character of, 134, 135
  Mugabe and, 120, 136
  ZAPU and, 120, 132
Nkrumah, Kwame, 132
Nogomo, Mutapa, *47*
nutrition, 178, 190, 202–5
Nyamahita, 37
Nyamazana, 51
Nyaminyami, river god, 26

Nyanga Mountains, 8, 17
Nyasaland, 81, 93, 94. *See also* Malawi.

Operation Noah, 26

Patriotic Front, 101, 120, 130. *See also*
  ZAPU-PF.
Pearce Commission, 101, 108–11,
  110
plateau, 7, 10, 14, 32–34
poaching, 152, 153
poetry, 208–12, 214, 215
  praise, 209–12, *213*
polygamy, 197
population, xii, 18, 20
Portuguese, 12, 33, 34, 41, 43–48, *45*,
  210
praise names, 38, 209
protected villages, 112, 113, *113*, 114
rainfall, xiii, 5, 7, 10, 13, 20
religion, 38, 46, 67, 148, 186–89 *See also*
  Christianity.
rhinoceros 152
  Rhino Survival Campaign, 152
Rhodes, Cecil John, 16, 18, *23*, 26, *71*,
  102, 123, *123*
  character of, 67, 68, 70–73, 85
  Rudd Concession and, 67–69
Rhodes Scholarships, 73
Rhodesia, 99–120
  blacks in, 105, 106, 108, 112, 115–
   17
  Northern, 81, 93, 94. *See also* Zambia.
  sanctions and, 99–101, 104
  Southern, 81, 91, 94–96, 99, 123
  whites in, 104, 105, 108, 113, 114, 117
Rhodesian Bantu Voters' Association
  (RBVA), 96
Rhodesian Front (RF), 81, 97
"Rhodesian Lullaby" (Eppel), 217
"Rhodesians Never Die" (Tholett), 106
river systems, 22–29
Roman Dutch Law, 184
Rozvi, 33, 49, 51, 60
Rudd, Charles, 68, *69*
Rudd Concession, 53, 67–69

Sabi River, xii, 22, 28, 29
Salisbury, 18, 74, 78, 80–85, 94, 98, 109,
    117. *See also* Harare.
savanna, 7, 10, 13, 20
sculpture. *See* Shona, sculpture of.
Selous, Frederick Courteney, 74, 83
Selous Scouts, 115
servants, 87–89, 104
Shaka, 57, 58
Shangani River, 7, 72
Shippard, Sir Sydney, 68
Shiri ya Mwari. *See* Zimbabwe birds.
shirichena. *See* Zimbabwe birds.
Shona, 10, 29, 50, 62
    customs of, 185–206
    language, 7, 34, 200, 201, 214
    names, 132, 194, 195
    Ndebele and, 60–62, 67, 130–32
    oral traditions of, 34, 36–39
    politics of, 97, 132
    pre-colonial history, 30–51
    rebellion, 75, 80, 84, 85–87, 88
    sculpture of, 30, 208, 215, 218–20, 218
    states, 16, 35, 39–51
Sibanda, Gloria, 216
Sithole, Rev. Ndabaningi, 97, 117
sjambok (hide whip), 83, 89
sleeping sickness, 12
Smith, Ian Douglas, 81, 97, 100, 101,
    103, 121, 128, 131
    black nationalism and, 104, 108, 115,
        117, 120
    British government and, 99, 108
    CAZ and, 105, 130
    character of, 102–5
    Kissinger and, 104, 120
    UDI and, 98, 99
    white Rhodesians and, 99, 102, 113,
        130
socialism, 126, 127, 132, 142, 146, 151,
    167
Sofala, 33, 43
soil erosion, 20, 21, 92, 149, 165
South Africa, 8, 13, 55, 70, 72, 117, 129,
    131, 132
    raids into Zimbabwe, 141
    Zimbabwe's economic dependence on,
        145, 160, 162

Southern African Development Coordination
    Conference, 162
Southern Rhodesian African National
    Congress, 97
spirit guardians. *See* ancestral spirits.
spirit mediums (*n'anga*, *svikiro*), 36–37, 38,
    86, 114, 171–74, 172, 173
svikiro. *See* spirit mediums.

Tanzania, 13, 117, 162
Tazara railway, 162
Tekere, Edgar, 137
temperatures, xiii, 10, 14, 20
Tengenenge Sculpture Community, 219
Thatcher, Margaret, 121
tobacco, 13, 100, 128, 144, 146
Todd, Sir Garfield, 81, 139
Torwa state, 32, 33, 48
totems, 35, 38, 191
tourism, 18, 22, 28, 145
townships, 88, 95, 105, 159
trade.
    exports and imports, 144, 145, 160
    precolonial, 12, 39, 40, 41, 43, 53,
        62
    See also economic sanctions.
Tribal Trust Lands, 105, 131, 137
tsetse fly, 10, 153
Tumbare, Torwa, 48

Umtali. *See* Mutare.
unemployment, 124–26, 158, 160
Unilateral Declaration of Independence
    (UDI), 99, 100
United African National Council (UANC),
    101
United Nations, 100, 101
United Nations Children's Fund, 176
urban life, 198–202

Vale, Dr. Glyn, 153
Vambe, Lawrence, 85
Victoria, Queen, 69, 82
Victoria Falls, 22–26, 23, 24
Voortrekkers, 57–59

Vukuzenzele cooperative, 139
Vumba Mountains, 17, 18

wages, 147, 159, 178
Waiting for the Rain (Mungoshi), 215
Whitehead, Edgar, 81, 95
whites, Rhodesia and, 104, 105, 108, 113,
    114, 117
    Zimbabwe and, 126, 129, 130, 137,
        138, 146, 147
Wildlife Producers' Association, 154
Wilson, Harold, 99, 108
Wilson, Major Allan, 7, 72, 73
witchcraft, 175, 183
women, 149
    city life and, 198
    industry and, 161
    law and, 182, 183

Youth League, 96

Zaire, 34, 95
Zambezi Escarpment, 20
Zambezi River, xii, 8, 20, 22–28, 34, 68,
    152, 153
    as political symbol, 70, 106
    Shona mythology and, 38, 185

Zambezi Valley, 9, 12, 20, 41, 48,
    152
Zambia, 8, 13, 22, 97, 145, 153. *See also*
    Rhodesia, Northern.
    Rhodesia and, 28, 93, 117, 177
ZANU (Zimbabwe African National Union),
    97, 111, 120, 133, 135
ZANU-PF (Zimbabwe African National
    Union—Patriotic Front), xiii, 97, 101,
    123, 126, 128, 130, 132, 136–7, 140,
    143
ZAPU (Zimbabwe African People's Union),
    97, 120, 132–36
Zhanta, Shona chief, *84*
zimbabwe (pl.: *mazimbabwe*), 16, 39, 48
"Zimbabwe" (Sibanda), 216
Zimbabwe African National Liberation
    Army (ZANLA), 111, *112*
Zimbabwe African National Union. *See*
    ZANU.
Zimbabwe African National
    Union—Patriotic Front. *See* ZANU-PF.
Zimbabwe African People's Union. *See*
    ZAPU.
Zimbabwe birds, 30, 41–43, *42*, 220
Zimbabwe Foundation for Education and
    Production (ZIMFEP), 167, 168
Zimbabwe People's Revolutionary Army
    (ZIPRA), 132, 133
Zimbabwe Project, 139